Photographer • Jarek Duk
Designer • Georgia Farrell
Art Direction & Stylist • Georgina Brant
Hair & Make Up • Zoe Kramer
Graphic Layout • Quail Studio
Model • BMA Model Management

First published in Great Britain in 2017 by
Quail Publishing Limited
The Old Forge, Market Square, Toddington,
Bedfordshire, LU5 6BP
E-mail: info@quailstudio.co.uk

Produced by quail studio

British Library Cataloguing in Publication Data -
Quail Publishing

Inspired Knits
ISBN: 978-0-9935908-2-5

INSPIRED
KNITS

by Georgia Farrell

12 HAND KNIT DESIGNS INFLUENCED BY
ARCHITECTURAL DETAILS AND SHAPES

Contents

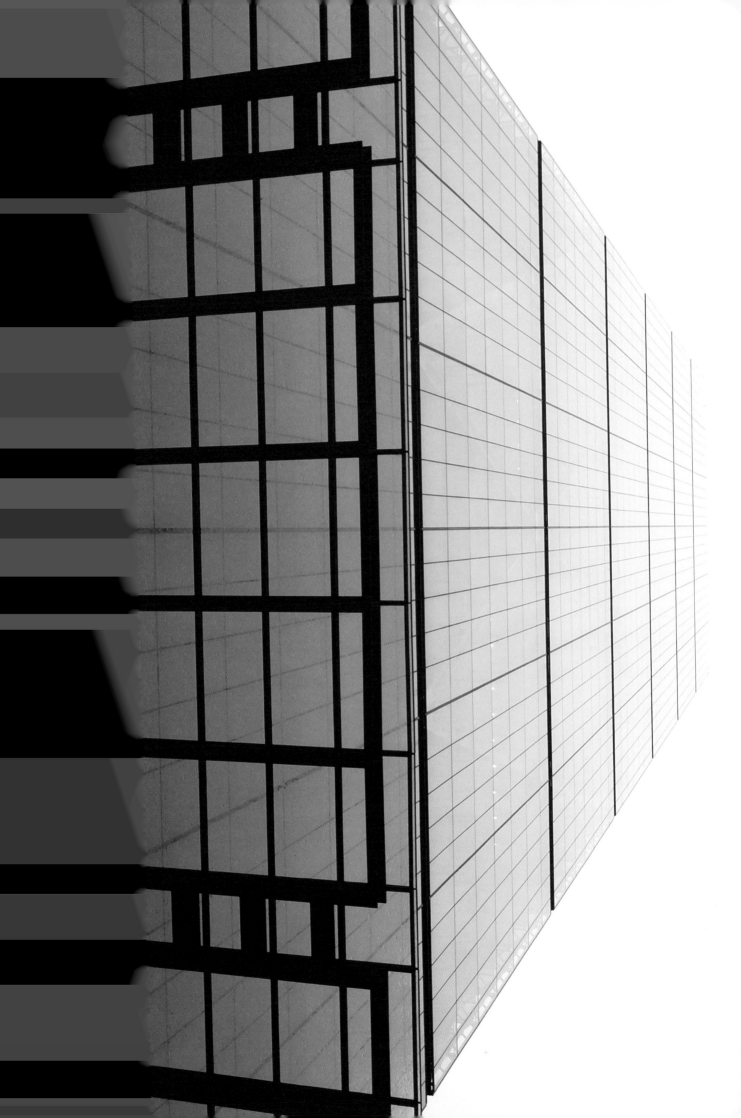

GEORGIA FARRELL

Georgia Farrell is a British
hand knitting designer
with a passion for modern
architecture. Translating
geometric patterns, shapes and
lines from buildings, into
textured stitch patterns and
then blending these textiles
with a modern fashion-led
aesthetic of clean lines and
simple details to create
striking, modern knitwear.

"Like a lot of people, my nan
taught me to knit when I was
young, but I just didn't have
the patience for it then, I
was terrible! I picked it up
again at college and went on
to study Textile Design at
university, but I would say
it wasn't until I was in my twenties, after I graduated,
that I got into hand knitting properly, and I've hardly
put the needles down since, I'm still an excited knitter
at heart!"

Whilst studying for her degree in Textile Design in
London, Georgia developed a great love for architecture
which directly influenced her design style and is still
the single biggest source of inspiration for her
work today.

Combining her love of hand knitting and her background
in textile design, Georgia now works out of her
design studio in Essex where she lives, creating
architecturally inspired knitting on a daily basis.

But, whenever possible, she loves to go looking for new
buildings to inspire her work, whether that's on her
doorstep in the City of London or travelling abroad.
Never without a camera, sketchbook, yarn and needles;
she could spend days wandering cities looking for
buildings and designing on the go.

Website - www.georgiafarrell.co.uk

Instagram - @georgiafarrelldesign

Twitter - @GeorgiaLFarrell

Pinterest - Georgia Farrell Design

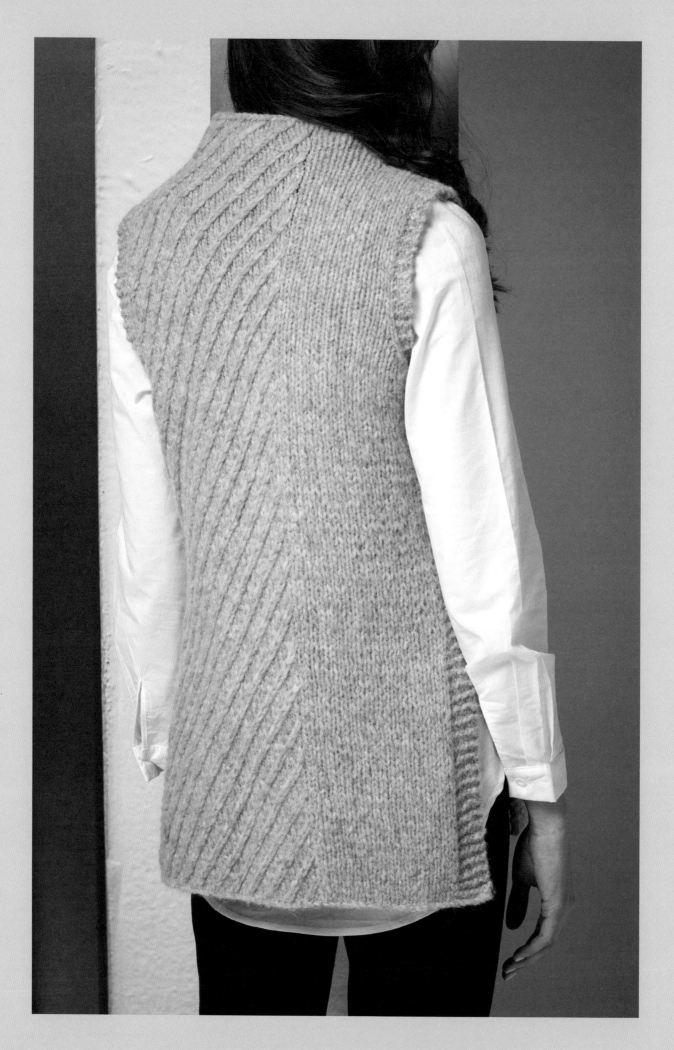

CHRYSLER - BOBBLE HAT

N.Y. - LONGLINE COATIGAN

THE
PATTERNS

315°

SLEEVELESS PULLOVER

This sleek sleeveless pullover is all about clean lines and angles. Knitted in four pieces and seamed, it features an off centre block of diagonal cabled lines against blocks of clean stocking stitch, all set off with neat design details.

SIZE

	S	M	L	XL	
To fit bust					
	81–86	91–97	102–107	112–117	cm
	32–34	36–38	40–42	44–46	in

Actual bust measurement of garment

94	102	111	120	cm
37	40	43½	47	in

YARN
Brushed Fleece

6	6	7	7	x 50gm

(photographed in Cairn 263)

NEEDLES
1 pair 6mm (no 4) (US 10) needles
Cable needle

TENSION
13 sts and 19 rows to 10cm measured over st st, 15 sts and 23 rows to 10cm measured over patt, both using 6mm (US 10) needles.

SPECIAL ABBREVIATIONS
C2B = slip next st onto cable needle and leave at back of work, K1, then K1 from cable needle; **C2F** = slip next st onto cable needle and leave at front of work, K1, then K1 from cable needle; **Sl 1p wyif** = slip 1 stitch purlwise with yarn in front (**WS** of work).

LEFT BACK
Using 6mm (US 10) needles cast on 46(50,54,58) sts.
Foundation row 1 (RS): Knit.
Foundation row 2: K6, Sl 1p, wyif (see special abbreviation), *P3, Sl 1p wyif, rep from * to last 3 sts, P3.
Row 1 (RS): K2, *C2B, K2, rep from * to last 8 sts, C2B, K6.
Row 2: K6, P1, Sl 1p wyif, *P3, Sl 1p wyif, rep from * to last 2 sts, P2.
Row 3: K1, *C2B, K2, rep from * to last 9 sts, C2B, K7.
Row 4: K6, P2, Sl 1p wyif, *P3, Sl 1p wyif, rep from * to last st, P1.
Row 5: K4, *C2B, K2, rep from * to last 6 sts, K6.
Row 6: K6, P3, Sl 1p wyif, *P3, Sl 1p wyif, rep from * to last 4 sts, P4.
Row 7: K3, *C2B, K2, rep from * to last 7 sts, K7.
Row 8: K6, Sl 1p wyif, *P3, Sl 1p wyif, rep from * to last 3 sts, P3.
These 8 rows form patt.
Cont in patt until left back meas 49.5(50.5,51.5,52.5) cm, ending with **WS** facing for next row.

Shape armhole
Keeping patt correct, cast off 3 sts at beg of next row. 43[47,51,55] sts.
Next row (RS): Patt to last 5 sts, K2tog, K3. 42[46,50,54]sts.
Next row: K3, P2tog, patt to end. 41[45,49,53]sts.
Working all armhole decreases as set by last 2 rows, dec 1 st at armhole edge of next

1(3,3,3) rows, then on foll 2(2,3,4) alt rows, then on foll 4th row. 37[39,42,45] sts. Cont straight until armhole meas 20(21,22,23) cm, ending with **WS** facing for next row.

Shape shoulder
Cast off 5(6,7,8) sts at beg of next and 4(5,6,8) sts at beg of foll alt row. 28[28,29,29] sts.
Work 4 rows straight.

Shape back neck
Next row (RS): Patt to last 3 sts, K2tog, K1. 27[27,28,28] sts.
Work 3 rows straight.
Next row: Patt to last 3 sts, K2tog, K1.
Work 5 rows straight. Cast off rem 26(26,27,27) sts.

RIGHT BACK
Using 6mm (US 10) needles cast on 25(27,29,32) sts.
Row 1 (RS): Knit.
Row 2: P to last 6 sts, K6.
These 2 rows set the sts — side edge 6 sts in g st with all other sts in st st.
Keeping sts correct as set, cont as folls:
Cont straight until right back meas 49.5(50.5,51.5,52.5) cm, ending with RS facing for next row.

Shape armhole
Cast off 3 sts at beg of next row. 22[24,26,29] sts.
Work 1 row.
Next row (RS): K3, Sl 1, K1, Psso, K to end. 21[23,25,28] sts.
Next row: P to last 5 sts, P2togtbl, K3. 20[22,24,27] sts.
Working all armhole decreases as set by last 2 rows, dec 1 st at armhole edge of next 1(3,3,3) rows, then on foll 1(0,1,2) alt rows, then on foll 4th row. 17[18,19,21] sts.
Cont straight until armhole meas 20(21,22,23) cm, ending with RS facing for next row.

Shape shoulder
Cast off 4(5,5,6) sts at beg of next and foll 1(0,0,0) alt row, then — (4,4,5) sts at beg of foll — (1,1,1) alt row. 9[9,10,10] sts.
Work 2 rows straight.

Shape back neck
Next row (RS): K1, Sl 1, K1, Psso, K to end. 8[8,9,9] sts.
Work 3 rows straight.
Next row: K1, Sl 1, K1, Psso, K to end. 7[7,8,8] sts.
Work 4 rows straight.
Cast off rem 7(7,8,8) sts purlwise.

LEFT FRONT
Using 6mm (US 10) needles cast on 46(50,54,58) sts.
Foundation row 1 (RS): Knit.
Foundation row 2: *P3, Sl 1p wyif, rep from * to last 6 sts, K6.
Row 1 (RS): K6, *C2F, K2, rep from * to end.
Row 2: P2, Sl 1p wyif, *P3, Sl 1p wyif, rep from * to last 7 sts, P1, K6.
Row 3: K7, *C2F, K2, rep from * to last 3 sts, C2F, K1.
Row 4: P1, Sl 1p wyif, *P3, Sl 1p wyif, rep from * to last 8 sts, P2, K6.
Row 5: K8, *C2F, K2, rep from * to last 2 sts, K2.
Row 6: P1, *P3, Sl 1p wyif, rep from * to last 9 sts, P3, K6.
Row 7: K9, *C2F, K2, rep from * to last st, K1.
Row 8: *P3, Sl 1p wyif, rep from * to last 6 sts, K6.
These 8 rows form patt.
Cont in patt until left front meas 49.5(50.5,51.5,52.5) cm, ending with RS facing for next row.

Shape armhole
Keeping patt correct, cast off 3 sts at beg of next row. 43[47,51,55] sts.
Work 1 row.
Next row (RS): K3, Sl 1, K1, Psso, patt to end.
Next row: Patt to last 5 sts, P2togtbl, K3.
Working all armhole decreases as set by last 2 rows, dec 1 st at armhole edge of next 1(3,3,3) rows, then on foll 2(2,3,4) alt rows, then on foll 4th row. 37[39,42,45] sts.
Cont straight until armhole meas 20(21,22,23) cm, ending with RS facing for next row.

Shape shoulder
Cast off 5(6,7,8) sts at beg of next and 4(5,6,8) sts at beg of foll alt row. 28[28,29,29] sts.
Work 4 rows straight.

Shape back neck
Next row (RS): K1, Sl 1, K1, Psso, patt to end.
Work 3 rows straight.
Next row: K1, Sl 1, K1, Psso, patt to end. 26[26,27,27] sts.
Work 5 rows straight. Cast off rem 26[26,27,27] sts.

RIGHT FRONT
Using 6mm (US 10) needles cast on
25(27,29,32) sts.
Row 1 (RS): Knit.
Row 2: K6, P to end.
These 2 rows set the sts — side edge 6 sts in
g st with all other sts in st st.
Keeping sts correct as set, cont as folls:
Cont straight until right front meas
49.5(50.5,51.5,52.5) cm, ending with **WS**
facing for next row.

Shape armhole
Cast off 3 sts at beg of next row.
22[24,26,29] sts.
Next row (RS): K to last 5 sts, K2tog, K3.
Next row: K3, P2tog, P to end.
Working all armhole decreases as set by last
2 rows, dec 1 st at armhole edge of next
1(3,3,3) rows, then on foll 1(0,1,2) alt
rows, then on foll 4ᵗʰ row. 17[18,19,21] sts.
Cont straight until armhole meas 20(21,22,23) cm,
ending with **WS** facing for next row.

Shape shoulder
Cast off 4(5,5,6) sts at beg of next and foll
1(0,0,0) alt row, then — (4,4,5) sts at beg
of foll — (1,1,1) alt row. 9[9,10,10] sts.
Work 2 rows straight.

Shape back neck
Next row (RS): K to last 3 sts, K2tog, K1.
8[8,9,9] sts.
Work 3 rows straight.
Next row: K to last 3 sts, K2tog, K1.
Work 4 rows straight. Cast off rem
7[7,8,8] sts purlwise.

MAKING UP
Press as described on the information page.
Using back stitch, or mattress stitch if
preferred, join left back and right back
together to form one piece, left front and
right front together to form one piece.
Join shoulder and neck seams.
Join side seams 25cm, 9½in up from
lower edge.

See information page for finishing
instructions.

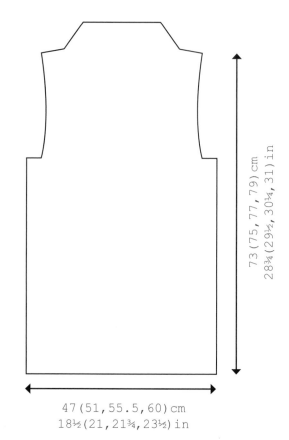

73 (75, 77, 79) cm
28¾ (29½, 30¾, 31) in

47 (51, 55.5, 60) cm
18½ (21, 21¾, 23½) in

BARBICAN

JACKET

The Barbican Estate is one of my favourite places in London and this jacket is basically a tribute to the architecture and to the place. Strong vertical columns rise up crossing more subtle horizontal blocks over this kimono inspired jacket, modernised with slimmed down long sleeves and finished with a triangular trim reminiscent of the balconies of the Barbican blocks.

SIZE

	S	M	L	XL	
To fit bust					
	81-86	91-97	102-107	112-117	cm
	32-34	36-38	40-42	44-46	in

Actual bust measurement of garment

113	123	133	143	cm
44½	48½	52½	56	in

YARN
Hemp tweed

14	15	17	18	x 50gm

(photographed in Pumice 138)

NEEDLES
1 pair 4mm (no 8) (US 6) needles

EXTRAS
Stitch markers.

TENSION
24 sts and 36 rows to 10cm measured over patt, using 4mm (US 6) needles.

SPECIAL ABBREVIATION
Sl 1p wyif = slip 1 stitch purlwise with yarn in front (**WS** of work).

BACK
Using 4mm (US 6) needles cast on 137 [149: 161: 173] sts.

Row 1 (RS): K0(5,0,5), P6(7,6,7), *K5, P7, rep from * to last 11(5,11,5)sts, K5, P6(0,6,0).

Row 2: K6(0,6,0), (Sl 1p wyif, P3, Sl 1p wyif) 1(0,1,0) times, (P4, Sl 1p wyif) 0(1,0,1) times, * K7, Sl 1p wyif, P3, Sl 1p wyif, rep from * to last 6(12,6,12) sts, K6(7,6,7), (Sl 1p, wyif, P4) 0(1,0,1) times.
Rows 3 and 4: As rows 1 and 2.
Row 5: Knit.
Row 6: P6(0,6,0), (Sl 1p wyif, P3, Sl 1p wyif) 1(0,1,0) times, (P4, Sl 1p wyif) 0(1,0,1) times, * K7, Sl 1p wyif, P3, Sl 1p wyif, rep from * to last 6(12,6,12) sts, P6(7,6,7), (Sl 1p, wyif, P4) 0(1,0,1) times.
Row 7: As row 5.
Row 8: As row 6.
These 8 rows form patt.
Cont in patt until back meas 42(44,46,48) cm, ending with RS facing for next row.

Shape shoulders
Keeping patt correct, cast off 2 sts at beg of next 64(52,40,28) rows, then —(3,3,3) sts at beg of next —(12,24,36) rows.
Cast off rem 9 sts.

LEFT FRONT
Using 4mm (US 6) needles cast on 67(73,79,85) sts.
Row 1 (RS): K0(5,0,5), P6(7,6,7), *K5, P7, rep from * to last st, P1.
Row 2: K1, *K7, Sl 1p wyif, P3, Sl 1p wyif, rep from * to last 6(12,6,12) sts, K6(7,6,7), (Sl 1p, wyif, P4) 0(1,0,1) times.
Rows 3 and 4: As rows 1 and 2.
Row 5: Knit.
Row 6: P8, Sl 1p wyif, P3, Sl 1p wyif, * K7,

Sl 1p wyif, P3, Sl 1p wyif, rep from * to last 6(12,6,12) sts, P6(7,6,7), (Sl 1p, wyif, P4) 0(1,0,1) times.

Row 7: As row 5.
Row 8: As row 6.
These 8 rows form patt.
Cont in patt until left front meas 42(44,46,48) cm, ending with **RS** facing for next row.

Shape shoulder
Cast off 2 sts at beg of next and foll 31(25,19,13) alt row, then —(3,3,3) sts at beg of foll —(6,12,18) alt rows.
Cast off rem 3 sts.

RIGHT FRONT
Using 4mm (US 6) needles cast on 67(73,79,85) sts.
Row 1 (RS): P8, *K5, P7, rep from * to last 11(5,11,5) sts, K5, P6(0,6,0).
Row 2: K6(0,6,0), (Sl 1p wyif, P3, Sl 1p wyif) 1(0,1,0) times, (P4, Sl 1p wyif) 0(1,0,1) times, * K7, Sl 1p wyif, P3, Sl 1p wyif, rep from * to last 8 sts, K8.
Rows 3 and 4: As rows 1 and 2.
Row 5: Knit.
Row 6: P6(0,6,0), (Sl 1p wyif, P3, Sl 1p wyif) 1(0,1,0) times, (P4, Sl 1p wyif) 0(1,0,1) times, * K7, Sl 1p wyif, P3, Sl 1p wyif, rep from * to last 8 sts, P8.
Row 7: As row 5.
Row 8: As row 6.
These 8 rows form patt.
Cont in patt until right front meas 42(44,46,48) cm, ending with **WS** facing for next row.

Shape shoulder
Cast off 2 sts at beg of next and foll 31(25,19,13) alt row, then — (3,3,3) sts at beg of foll —(6,12,18) alt rows.
Cast off rem 3 sts purlwise.

SLEEVES (make two the same)
Using 4mm (US 6) needles cast on 41(43,47,47) sts.
Row 1 (RS): P6(7,3,3), *K5, P7, rep from * to last 11(12,8,8)sts, K5, P6(7,3,3).
Row 2: K6(7,3,3), Sl 1p wyif, P3, Sl 1p wyif, * K7, Sl 1p wyif, P3, Sl 1p wyif, rep from * to last 6(7,3,3) sts, K6(7,3,3).
Rows 3 and 4: As rows 1 and 2.
Row 5: Knit.
Row 6: P6(7,3,3), Sl 1p wyif, P3, Sl 1p wyif, * K7, Sl 1p wyif, P3, Sl 1p wyif, rep from * to last 6(7,3,3) sts, P6(7,3,3).
Row 7: As row 5.
Row 8: As row 6.
These 8 rows form patt.
Cont in patt, shaping sides by inc 1 st at

each end of next and every foll 8th(8th,8th,6th) row to 59(69,79,59) sts, then on every foll 10th(10th,10th,8th) row until there are 75(79,85,89) sts, taking inc sts into patt.
Cont straight until sleeve meas 45(46,47,47) cm, ending with RS facing for next row.

Shape top
Cast off 8(8,9,10)sts at beg of next 6(2,4,6) rows, -(9,10, -) sts at beg of next — (4,2, -) rows.
Cast off rem 27(27,29,29) sts.

MAKING UP
Press as described on the information page. Join shoulder seams using back stitch, or mattress stitch if preferred. Place markers along side seam edges of back and fronts 16(17,18,19)cm either side of shoulder seams (to denote armhole openings). Sew in sleeves. Join side and sleeve seams.

BAND
Using 4mm (US 6) needles cast on 4 sts.
Knit 2 rows.
Work for patt as folls:
Row 1 (RS): K1, M1, K to end. 5 sts.
Row 2: Knit.
Rep rows 1 and 2 a further 4 times. 9 sts.
Row 11: Cast off 5 sts, K to end. 4 sts.
Row 12: Knit.
These 12 rows form patt.
Cont in patt until band, when slightly stretched, fits up left front opening edge, and down right front opening edge, ending with row 11 of patt. Cast off knitwise (on a **WS** row).
Slip stitch band in place.

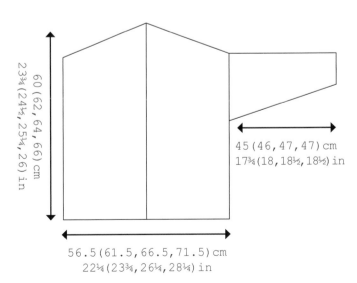

60 (62, 64, 66) cm
23¾ (24½, 25¼, 26) in

45 (46, 47, 47) cm
17¾ (18, 18½, 18½) in

56.5 (61.5, 66.5, 71.5) cm
22¼ (23¾, 26¼, 28¼) in

CHRYSLER

BOBBLE HAT

My Chrysler bobble hat is, of course, inspired by the iconic Chrylser building that has stood the test of time on the ever evolving New York skyline.

YARN

Pure Wool Superwash DK

A Seville 113

| | 1 | x 50gm |

B Flint 105

| | 1 | x 50gm |

or

Felted Tweed

A Seafarer 170

| | 1 | x 50gm |

B Granite 191

| | 1 | x 50gm |

NEEDLES

1 pair 3.75mm (no 9) (US 5) needles
1 pair 3.25mm (no 10) (US 3) needles

EXTRAS

Pompom maker (optional)

TENSION

25 sts and 32 rows to 10cm measured over patt, using 3.75mm (US 5) needles.

FINISHED SIZE

To fit an average size women's head

SPECIAL ABBREVIATIONS

Sl 1p wyif = slip 1 stitch purlwise with yarn in front (**WS** of work); **Sl 2tog** = insert needle into next 2 sts as if to k2tog and slip the 2 sts from the left-hand needle to right-hand needle without working them.

HAT

Using 3.25mm (US 3) needles and yarn A cast on 126 sts.

Row 1 (RS): K2, *P2, K2, rep from * to end.

Row 2: P2, *K2, P2, rep from * to end.

These 2 rows form rib.

Work in rib for a further 44 rows.

Break off yarn A, join in yarn B.

Change to 3.75mm needles.

Next row: K8, (K2tog, K16) 6 times, K2tog, K8. 119 sts.

Next row: Purl.

Chart Instructions;

Beg and ending rows as indicated, repeating the 13 st patt repeat 9 times across the row, work rows 1 - 36 once or work rows 1 - 36 from written instructions below.

Written Instructions;

Row 1 (RS): *K2, P1, K9, P1, rep from * to last 2 sts, K2.

Row 2: P2, *K1, P4, Sl 1p wyif, P4, K1, P2, rep from * to end.

Row 3: *K2, P2, K7, P2, rep from * to last 2 sts, K2.

Row 4: P2, *K2, P3, Sl 1p wyif, P3, K2, P2, rep from * to end.

Row 5: *K3, P2, K5, P2, K1, rep from * to last 2 sts, K2.

Row 6: P2, *P1, K2, P2, Sl 1p wyif, P2, K2, P3, rep from * to end.

Row 7: *(K3, P3) twice, K1, rep from * to last 2 sts, K2.

Row 8: P2, *P1, K3, P1, Sl 1p wyif, P1, K3, P3, rep from * to

Row 9: *K4, P3, K1, P3, K2, rep from * to last 2 sts, K2.

Row 10: P2, *P2, K3, Sl 1p wyif, K3, P4, rep from * to end.

Row 11: As row 9.

Row 12: As row 10.
Row 13: *K5, P2, K1, P2, K3, rep from * to last 2 sts, K2.
Row 14: P2, *P3, K2, Sl 1p wyif, K2, P5, rep from * to end.
Row 15: As row 13.
Row 16: As row 14.
Row 17: *K6, P1, K1, P1, K4, rep from * to last 2 sts, K2.
Row 18: P2, *P4, K1, Sl 1p wyif, K1, P6, rep from * to end.
Row 19: As row 17.
Row 20: As row 18.
Row 21: Knit.
Row 22: P2, *P5, Sl 1p wyif, P7, rep from * to end.
Rows 23 to 36: Rep rows 21 and 22, 7 times.

SHAPE TOP
Row 1 (RS): K6, Sl 2tog, K1, P2sso, *K10, Sl 2tog, K1, P2sso, rep from * to last 6 sts, K6. 101 sts.
Row 2: P6, Sl 1, *P10, Sl 1, rep from * to last 6 sts, P6.
Row 3: Knit.
Row 4: As row 2.
Row 5: K5, Sl 2tog, K1, P2sso, *K8, Sl 2tog, K1, P2sso, rep from * to last 5 sts, K5. 83 sts.
Row 6: P5, Sl 1, *P8, Sl 1, rep from * to last 5 sts, P5.
Row 7: Knit.
Row 8: As row 6.
Row 9: K4, Sl 2tog, K1, P2sso, *K6, Sl 2tog, K1, P2sso, rep from * to last 4 sts, K4. 65 sts.
Row 10: P4, Sl 1, *P6, Sl 1, rep from * to last 4 sts, P4.
Row 11: K3, Sl 2tog, K1, P2sso, *K4, Sl 2tog, K1, P2sso, rep from * to last 3 sts, K3. 47 sts.
Row 12: P3, Sl 1, *P4, Sl 1, rep from * to last 3 sts, P3.
Row 13: K2, Sl 2tog, K1, P2sso, *K2, Sl 2tog, K1, P2sso, rep from * to last 2 sts, K2. 29 sts.
Row 14: (P2, Sl 1) 9 times, P2.
Row 15: K1, *Sl 2tog, K1, P2sso, rep from * to last st, K1. 11 sts.
Row 16: Purl.

Break yarn and thread through rem 11 sts.
Pull up tight and fasten off securely.

MAKING UP
Press as described on the information page.
Join back seam, reversing sewing for turn back. Using yarn A, make a pompom and attach to centre of crown. See information page for finishing instructions.

CHART

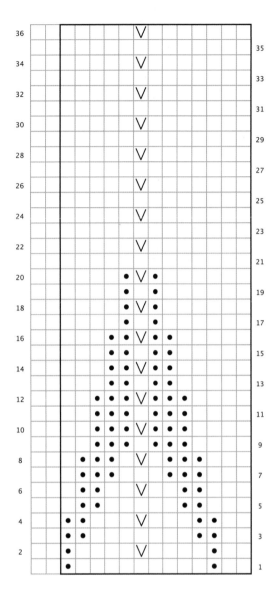

Key

RS: knit
WS: purl

• RS: purl
  WS: knit

V RS: slip
  WS: slip purlwise with yarn in front

Repeat

CONCRETE BLOCKS
LONG SLEEVED JUMPER

I have a great fondness for exposed concrete blocks used in architecture, and that was what influenced the simple asymmetric, positive negative blocks pattern that covers this classic jumper.

SIZE

	S	M	L	XL	
To fit bust					
	81-86	91-97	102-107	112-117	cm
	32-34	36-38	40-42	44-46	in

Actual bust measurement of garment

93	102	111	122	cm
36½	40	43½	48	in

YARN
Felted Tweed

7	8	9	9	x 50gm

(photographed in Alabaster 197)

NEEDLES
1 pair 4mm (no 8) (US 6) needles
4mm (no 8) (US 6) circular needle,
40cm long.

EXTRAS
Stitch holders.
Stitch markers.

TENSION
22 sts and 38 rows to 10cm measured over patt, using 4mm (US 6) needles.

BACK
Using 4mm (US 6) needles cast on 104(114,124,136) sts.
Work in g st for 6 rows, ending with RS facing for next row.

Now work in patt as folls:

Row 1 (RS): Knit.
Row 2: P18(21,23,26), K51(55,61,67), P35(38,40,43).
Rows 3 to 6: Rep rows 1 and 2, twice.
Row 7: Knit.
Row 8: K18(21,23,26), P51(55,61,67), K35(38,40,43).
Rows 9 to 12: Rep rows 7 and 8, twice.
These 12 rows form patt.
Cont in patt until back meas 33.5(34.5,35.5,36.5) cm, ending with RS facing for next row.

Shape armholes
Keeping patt correct, cast off 4(5,6,7) sts at beg of next 2 rows. 96[104,112,122] sts.
Dec 1 st at each end of next 3(5,5,5) rows, then on foll 2(2,3,4) alt rows, and 2 foll 4th rows. 82[86,92,100] sts.
Cont straight until armhole meas 19(20,21,22) cm, ending with RS facing for next row.

Shape shoulders
Cast off 3(3,4,4) sts at beg of next 2 rows. 76[80,84,92] sts.
Shape back neck
Next row (RS): Cast off 3(3,4,4) sts, patt until there are 12(14,14,18) sts on right needle and turn, leaving rem sts on a holder. Work each side of neck separately.
Dec 1 st at neck edge of 2nd and foll 4th rows, **and at same time** cast off 3(3,3,4) sts at beg of 2nd row and 1(2,2,2) foll alt row, then cast off 2 (-, -, -) sts on 1 (-, -, -) foll alt row.
Work 1 row.
Cast off rem 2(3,3,4) sts.

With RS facing, slip centre 46(46,48,48) sts onto a holder, rejoin yarn to rem sts and patt to end.
Complete to match first side, reversing shapings.

FRONT
Work as given for back until 10(10,14,14) rows less have been worked than on back to beg of shoulder shaping, ending with RS facing for next row.

Shape front neck
Keeping patt correct work as folls:
Next row (RS): Patt 25(27,30,34) and turn, leaving rem sts on a holder.
Work each side of neck separately.
Cast off 3 sts at beg of next row, 2 sts at beg of foll 2 alt rows and 1 st at beg of 2(2,3,3) foll alt rows, ending with RS facing for next row. 16[18,20,24] sts.
Work 0(0,2,2) rows straight.

Shape shoulder
Cast off 3(3,4,4) sts at beg of next and foll 3(4,1,4) alt rows, then 2(-, 3, -) sts at beg of foll 1(-, 3, -) alt rows.
Work 1 row. 2[3,3,4] sts.
Cast off rem 2(3,3,4) sts.
With RS facing, slip centre 32 sts onto a holder, rejoin yarn to rem sts and cast off 3 sts, patt to end. 22[24,27,31] sts.
Complete to match first side, reversing shapings.

SLEEVES (make two the same)
Using 4mm (US 6) needles cast on 52(54,56,56) sts.
Work in g st for 6 rows, ending with RS facing for next row.
Now work in patt as folls:
Row 1 (RS): Knit.
Row 2: P21, K10(12,14,14), P21.
Rows 3 to 6: Rep rows 1 and 2, twice.
Row 7: Knit.
Row 8: K21, P10(12,14,14), K21.
Rows 9 to 12: Rep rows 7 and 8, twice.
These 12 rows form patt.
Cont in patt as folls:
Inc 1 st at each end of 1st and every foll 14th(12th,12th,8th) row to 72(66,80,66) sts, then on every foll — (14th, -, 10th) row until there are — (76, -, 86) sts, taking inc sts into patt.
Cont straight until sleeve meas 43(44,45,45) cm, ending with RS facing for next row.

Shape top
Keeping patt correct, cast off 4(5,6,7) sts at beg of next 2 rows. 64[66,68,72] sts.
Dec 1 st at each end of next 3 rows, then on 2 foll alt rows, then on 6 foll 4th rows. 42[44,46,50] sts.

Work 1 row, ending with RS facing for next row.

For all sizes: Dec 1 st at each end of every foll alt row to 32 sts.
Dec 1 st at each end of foll 3 rows, ending with RS facing for next row. 26 sts.
Cast off 4 sts at beg of next 4 rows.
Cast off rem 10 sts.

MAKING UP
Press as described on the information page.
Join shoulder seams using back stitch, or mattress stitch if preferred.

Neckband
With RS facing and using 4mm (US 6) circular needle, pick up and knit 21(21,23,23) sts down left side of front neck, K across 32 sts on front holder, pick up and knit 21(21,23,23) sts up right side of front neck, 8 sts down right side of back neck, K across 46(46,48,48) sts on back holder, pick up and knit 8 sts up right side of back neck. 136[136,142,142] sts.
Place marker to mark beg of round.
Round 1: Purl.
Round 2: Knit.
Rep rounds 1 and 2, twice more. Cast off.

Sew in sleeves.
Join side and sleeve seams.
See information page for finishing instructions.

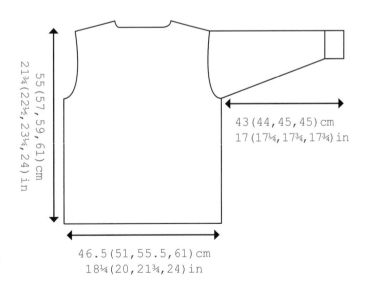

55(57,59,61) cm
21¾(22½,23¼,24) in

43(44,45,45) cm
17(17¼,17¾,17¾) in

46.5(51,55.5,61) cm
18¼(20,21¾,24) in

N.Y.

LONGLINE COATIGAN

On a trip to New York a few years ago I was able to visit Norman Foster's iconic Hearst Tower which inspired the textured tessellating triangles that cover this chunky, longline coatigan.

SIZE

	S	M	L	XL	
To fit bust					
	81-86	91-97	102-107	112-117	cm
	32-34	36-38	40-42	44-46	in

Actual bust measurement of garment

98	110	118	130	cm
38½	43½	46½	51	in

YARN
Big Wool
A Concrete 061

4	4	4	4	x 100gm

B Surf 081

7	8	9	10	x 100gm

NEEDLES
1 pair 9mm (no 00) (US 13) needles

EXTRAS
Stitch holders

TENSION
10 sts and 18 rows to 10cm measured over small texture patt (Chart A), 10 sts and 17 rows to 10cm measured over large texture patt (Chart B), both using 9mm (US 13) needles.

BACK
Using 9mm (US 13) needles and yarn A, cast on 51(57,61,67) sts.
Work in g st for 8 rows, ending with RS facing for next row.
Beg and ending rows as indicated, cont in patt from chart A for body as folls:
Work chart rows 1 to 12.
Now rep chart rows 1 to 12, 3 more times.
Break off yarn A, join in yarn B.
Beg and ending rows as indicated and repeating the 24 row patt rep throughout, now work in patt from Chart B as folls:
Cont in patt until back meas 63(64,65,66)cm, ending with RS facing for next row.

Shape armholes
Keeping patt correct, cast off 2(2,3,3) sts at beg of next 2 rows. 47[53,55,61] sts.
Dec 1 st at each end of next 3(3,3,5) rows, then on foll 1(3,3,2) alt rows. 39[41,43,47] sts.
Cont straight until armhole meas 20(21,22,23) cm, ending with RS facing for next row.

Shape shoulder and back neck
Next row (RS): Cast off 3(3,3,4) sts, patt until there are 9(10,10,11) sts on right needle and turn, leaving rem sts on a holder. Work each side of neck separately.
Cast off 1 st at neck edge in next and foll alt row, **and at same time** cast off 3(4,4,4) sts at beg of 2nd row, ending with RS facing for next row. 4[4,4,5] sts.
Cast off rem 4(4,4,5) sts.
With RS facing, slip centre 15(15,17,17) sts onto a holder, rejoin yarn to rem sts and cast off 1 st, patt to end. 11[12,12,14] sts.

Complete to match first side, reversing shapings.

LEFT FRONT

Using 9mm (US 13) needles and yarn A, cast on 28(31,33,36) sts.

Work in g st for 8 rows, ending with RS facing for next row.

Now work 2 sts at front edge in g st and place chart A as folls:

Row 1 (RS): Work 26(29,31,34) sts as row 1 of chart A, K2.

Row 2: K2, work next 26(29,31,34) sts as row 2 of chart A.

These 2 rows set the sts - 26[29,31,34] sts in patt from chart A with 2 sts at front edge worked in g st.

Keeping sts correct as now set, work a further 46 rows.

Break off yarn A, join in yarn B.

Now work 2 sts at front edge in g st and place chart B as folls:

Row 1 (RS): Work 26(29,31,34) sts as row 1 of chart B, K2.

Row 2: K2, work next 26(29,31,34) sts as row 2 of chart B.

These 2 rows set the sts — 26(29,31,34) sts in patt from chart B with 2 sts at front edge worked in g st.

Keeping sts correct as now set throughout, cont as folls:

Cont in patt until left front meas 63(64,65,66) cm, ending with RS facing for next row.

Shape armhole

Keeping patt correct, cast off 2(2,3,3) sts at beg of next row. 26[29,30,33] sts.

Work 1 row.

Dec 1 st at armhole edge of next 3(3,3,5) rows, then on foll 1(3,3,2) alt rows. 22[23,24,26] sts.

Cont straight until 8(8,10,10) rows less have been worked than on back to beg of shoulder shaping, ending with RS facing for next row.

Shape front neck

Next row (RS): Patt 15(16,17,19) sts and turn, leaving rem 7 sts on a holder (for neckband).

Keeping patt correct, cast off 2 sts at neck edge in next row, cast off 1 st at neck edge in foll 3(3,4,4) alt row. 10[11,11,13] sts.

Shape shoulder

Cast off 3(3,3,4) sts at beg of next row, then 3(4,4,4) sts at beg of foll alt row.

Work 1 row.

Cast off rem 4(4,4,5) sts.

RIGHT FRONT

Using 9mm (US 13) needles and yarn A, cast on 28(31,33,36) sts.

Work in g st for 8 rows, ending with RS facing for next row.

Now work 2 sts at front edge in g st and place chart A as folls:

Row 1 (RS): K2, work next 26(29,31,34) sts as row 1 of chart A.

Row 2: Work 26(29,31,34) sts as row 2 of chart A, K2.

These 2 rows set the sts — 26(29,31,34) sts in patt from chart A with 2 sts at front edge worked in g st.

Keeping sts correct as now set, work a further 46 rows.

Break off yarn A, join in yarn B.

Now work 2 sts at front edge in g st and place chart B as folls:

Row 1 (RS): K2, work next 26(29,31,34) sts as row 1 of chart B.

Row 2: Work 26(29,31,34) sts as row 2 of chart B, K2.

These 2 rows set the sts — 26(29,31,34) sts in patt from chart B with 2 sts at front edge worked in g st.

Keeping sts correct as now set throughout, cont as folls:

Complete to match left front, reversing shapings and working first row of neck shaping as folls:

Next row (RS): Patt 7 sts and slip these sts onto a holder (for neckband), patt to end. 15[16,17,19] sts.

SLEEVES (make two the same)

Using 9mm (US 13) needles and yarn A, cast on 21 [21: 23: 23] sts.

Work in g st for 8 rows, ending with RS facing for next row.

Beg and ending rows as indicated, cont in patt from chart A for sleeve as folls:

Work chart rows 1 to 12.

Break off yarn A, join in yarn B.

Beg and ending rows as indicated and repeating the 24 row patt rep throughout, now work in patt from Chart B as folls:

Inc 1 st at each end of 1st and every foll 8th [6th: 6th: 6th] row to 35 [31: 31: 39] sts, then on every foll - [8th: 8th: 8th] row until there are - [37: 39: 41] sts, taking inc sts into patt. Cont straight until sleeve meas 43 [44: 45: 45] cm, ending with RS facing for next row.

Shape top

Keeping patt correct, cast off 2(2,3,3) sts at beg of next 2 rows. 31[33,33,35] sts.

Dec 1 st at each end of next 3 rows, then on foll 1(2,1,2) alt rows, then on 2(2,3,3) foll 4th rows. 19 sts.

Work 1 row, ending with RS facing for
next row.

For all sizes: Dec 1 st at each end of foll 2
rows. 15 sts.
Cast off 2 sts at beg of next 2 rows.   11 sts.
Cast off 3 sts at beg of next 2 rows.
Cast off rem 5 sts.

MAKING UP
Press as described on the information page.
Join both shoulder seams using back stitch,
or mattress stitch if preferred.

Neckband
With RS facing, using 9mm needles slip 7 sts
from right front holder onto right needle,
rejoin yarn and pick up and knit 6(6,7,7)
sts up right side of front neck, and 2 sts
down right side of back neck, K across
15(15,17,17) sts on back holder, pick up
and knit 2 sts up left side of back neck,
6(6,7,7) sts down left side of front neck,
then knit across 7 sts on left front holder.
45[45,49,49] sts.
Cast off knitwise (on **WS** row).

Sew in sleeves.
Join side and sleeve seams.

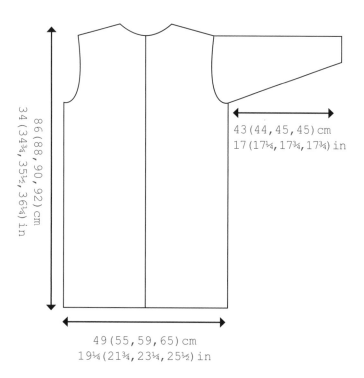

86(88, 90, 92) cm
34 (34¾, 35½, 36¼) in

43(44, 45, 45) cm
17(17¼, 17¾, 17¾) in

49(55, 59, 65) cm
19¼(21¾, 23¼, 25½) in

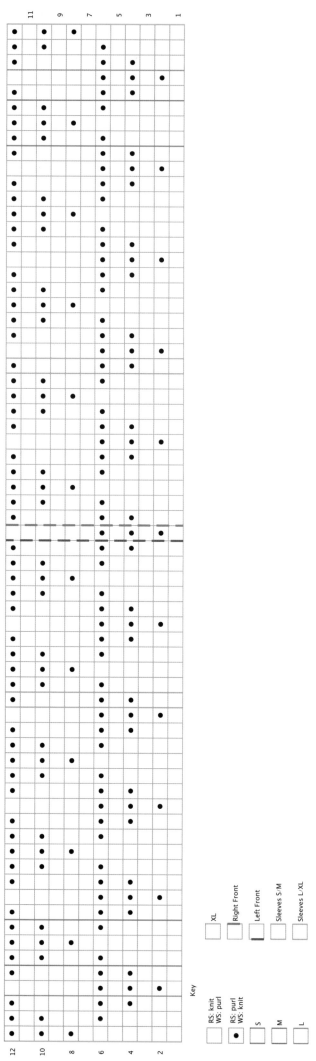

CHART A

Key

RS: knit
WS: purl

RS: purl
WS: knit

S
M
L

XL

Right Front

Left Front

Sleeves S/M

Sleeves L/XL

CHART B

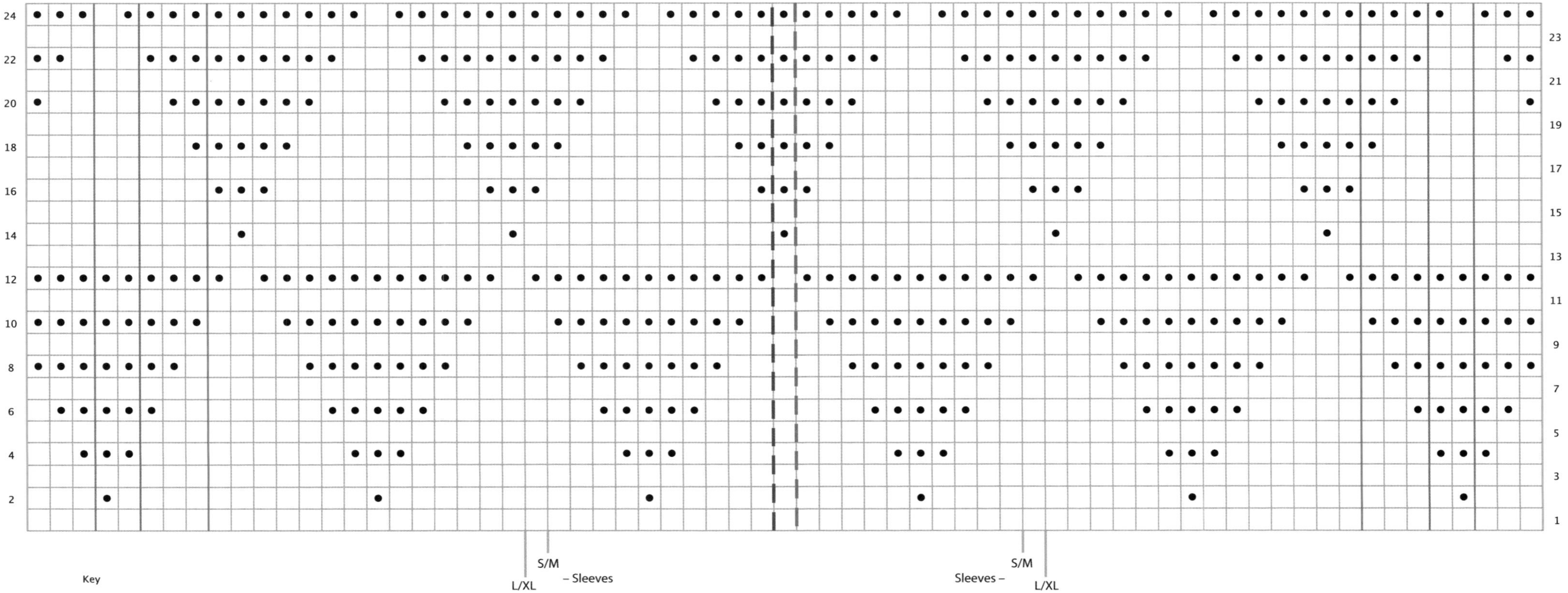

Sleeves – L/XL
S/M
Sleeves – L/XL / S/M
– Sleeves
S/M
L/XL

Key

RS: knit
WS: purl

RS: purl
WS: knit

S

M

L

XL

Right Front

Left Front

Sleeves S/M

Sleeves L/XL

51

TRAPEZIUM
WRAP & SCARF

*I love using geometric tessellating patterns
that I find as claddings for buildings or
building blocks, in my work, they translate
perfectly into knitted textured patterns like
the tessellating trapeziums that cover these
cosy winter accessories.*

YARN
WRAP
Kid Classic
            8   x 50gm
(photographed in Tattoo 856)

SCARF
Big Wool
            6   x 100gm
(photographed in Glum 056)

NEEDLES
WRAP
1 pair 4.5mm (no 7) (US 7) needles
SCARF
1 pair 9mm (no 00) (US 13) needles

TENSION
WRAP
21 sts and 32 rows to 10cm measured over patt
using 4.5mm (US 7) needles.
SCARF
10.5 sts and 16 rows to 10cm measured over
patt, using 9mm (US 13)

FINISHED SIZE
Completed wrap is approx. 62cm (24½in) wide
and 139cm (55in) long.
Completed scarf is approx. 34.5cm (13½in) and
(77in) long.

WRAP
Using 4.5mm (US 7) needles cast on 130 sts.
Row 1 (RS): *K1, P1, rep from * to end.
Row 2: *P1, K1, rep from * to end.
These 2 rows form moss st.
Work a further 4 rows in moss st.
Now work in patt as folls:

Row 1 (RS): (K1,P1) twice, K1, *K10, P10,
K10, rep from * to last 5 sts, (P1, K1)
twice, P1.
Row 2: (P1,K1) twice, P1, *P10, K10, P10, rep
from * to last 5 sts, (K1, P1) twice, K1.
Row 3: (K1,P1) twice, K1, *K9, P12, K9, rep
from * to last 5 sts, (P1, K1) twice, P1.
Row 4: (P1,K1) twice, P1, *P9, K12, P9, rep
from * to last 5 sts, (K1, P1) twice, K1.
Row 5: (K1,P1) twice, K1, *K8, P14, K8, rep
from * to last 5 sts, (P1, K1) twice, P1.
Row 6: (P1,K1) twice, P1, *P8, K14, P8, rep
from * to last 5 sts, (K1, P1) twice, K1.
Row 7: (K1,P1) twice, K1, *K7, P16, K7, rep
from * to last 5 sts, (P1, K1) twice, P1.
Row 8: (P1,K1) twice, P1, *P7, K16, P7, rep
from * to last 5 sts, (K1, P1) twice, K1.
Row 9: (K1,P1) twice, K1, *K6, P18, K6, rep
from * to last 5 sts, (P1, K1) twice, P1.
Row 10: (P1,K1) twice, P1, *P6, K18, P6, rep
from * to last 5 sts, (K1, P1) twice, K1.
Row 11: (K1,P1) twice, K1, *K5, P20, K5, rep
from * to last 5 sts, (P1, K1) twice, P1.
Row 12: (P1,K1) twice, P1, *P5, K20, P5, rep
from * to last 5 sts, (K1, P1) twice, K1.
Row 13: (K1,P1) twice, K1, *P5, K20, P5, rep
from * to last 5 sts, (P1, K1) twice, P1.
Row 14: (P1,K1) twice, P1, *K5, P20, K5, rep
from * to last 5 sts, (K1, P1) twice, K1.
Row 15: (K1,P1) twice, K1, *P6, K18, P6, rep
from * to last 5 sts, (P1, K1) twice, P1.
Row 16: (P1,K1) twice, P1, *K6, P18, K6, rep
from * to last 5 sts, (K1, P1) twice, K1.
Row 17: (K1,P1) twice, K1, *P7, K16, P7, rep
from * to last 5 sts, (P1, K1) twice, P1.
Row 18: (P1,K1) twice, P1, *K7, P16, K7, rep
from * to last 5 sts, (K1, P1) twice, K1.
Row 19: (K1,P1) twice, K1, *P8, K14, P8, rep

from * to last 5 sts, (P1, K1) twice, P1.
Row 20: (P1,K1) twice, P1, *K8, P14, K8, rep
from * to last 5 sts, (K1, P1) twice, K1.
Row 21: (K1,P1) twice, K1, *P9, K12, P9, rep
from * to last 5 sts, (P1, K1) twice, P1.
Row 22: (P1,K1) twice, P1, *K9, P12, K9, rep
from * to last 5 sts, (K1, P1) twice, K1.
Row 23: (K1,P1) twice, K1, *P10, K10, P10,
rep from * to last 5 sts, (P1, K1) twice, P1.
Row 24: (P1,K1) twice, P1, *K10, P10, K10,
rep from * to last 5 sts, (K1, P1) twice, K1.
These 24 rows form patt.
Cont in patt for a further 408 rows, ending
with RS facing for next row.
Work a further 6 rows in moss st.
Cast off in moss st.

MAKING UP
Press as described on the information page.

SCARF
Using 9mm (US 13) needles cast on 36 sts.
Row 1 (RS): *K1, P1, rep from * to end.
Row 2: *P1, K1, rep from * to end.
These 2 rows form moss st.
Work a further 2 rows in moss st.
Now work in patt as folls:
Row 1 (RS): K1,P1, K11, P10, K10, P1, K1, P1.
Row 2: P1, K1, P11, K10, P10, K1, P1, K1.
Row 3: K1, P1, K10, P12, K9, P1, K1, P1.
Row 4: P1, K1, P10, K12, P9, K1, P1, K1.
Row 5: K1, P1, K9, P14, K8, P1, K1, P1.
Row 6: P1, K1, P9, K14, P8, K1, P1, K1.
Row 7: K1, P1, K8, P16, K7, P1, K1, P1.
Row 8: P1, K1, P8, K16, P7, K1, P1, K1.
Row 9: K1, P1, K7, P18, K6, P1, K1, P1.
Row 10: P1, K1, P7, K18, P6, K1, P1, K1.
Row 11: K1, P1, K6, P20, K5, P1, K1, P1.
Row 12: P1, K1, P6, K20, P5, K1, P1, K1.
Row 13: K1, P1, K1, P5, K20, P6, K1, P1.
Row 14: P1, K1, P1, K5, P20, K6, P1, K1.
Row 15: K1, P1, K1, P6, K18, P7, K1, P1.
Row 16: P1, K1, P1, K6, P18, K7, P1, K1.
Row 17: K1, P1, K1, P7, K16, P8, K1, P1.
Row 18: P1, K1, P1, K7, P16, K8, P1, K1.
Row 19: K1, P1, K1, P8, K14, P9, K1, P1.
Row 20: P1, K1, P1, K8, P14, K9, P1, K1.
Row 21: K1, P1, K1, P9, K12, P10, K1, P1.
Row 22: P1, K1, P1, K9, P12, K10, P1, K1.
Row 23: K1, P1, K1, P10, K10, P11, K1, P1.
Row 24: P1, K1, P1, K10, P10, K11, P1, K1.
These 24 rows form patt.
Cont in patt for a further 288 rows, ending
with RS facing for next row.
Work a further 4 rows in moss st.
Cast off in moss st.

MAKING UP
Press as described on the information page.

WRAP

AXE

CROPPED JUMPER

Axe is inspired by a building you will all know; 30 St Mary Axe, more commonly known as 'The Gherkin'. A cropped jumper with contrast rib trims and an all over textured pattern of triangles and diagonal blocks influenced by the structure of the building.

SIZE

S	M	L	XL	
To fit bust				
81–86	91–97	102–107	112–117	cm
32–34	36–38	40–42	44–46	in

Actual bust measurement of garment

94	106	116	126	cm
37	41½	45½	49	in

YARN
Pure Wool Superwash dk
A Marl 104

6	7	8	9	x 50gm

B Caviar 114

1	1	1	1	x 50gm

NEEDLES
1 pair 3.5mm (no 4) (US 10/9) needles
1 pair 4mm (no 8) (US 6) needles

EXTRAS
Stitch holders

TENSION
24 sts and 33 rows to 10cm measured over patt, using 4mm (US 6) needles.

BACK
Using 3.5mm (US 10/9) needles and yarn B cast on 115(129,141,153) sts.
Row 1 (RS): K1, *P1, K1, rep from * to end.

Row 2: P1, *K1, P1, rep from * to end.
These 2 rows form rib.
Cont in rib until work meas 4cm, ending with RS facing for next row.
Break off yarn B and join in yarn A
Change to 4mm (US 6) needles.
Beg and ending rows as indicated, repeating the 16 st patt repeat 7(7,8,9) times across each row and repeating the 64 row patt repeat throughout, cont in patt from Chart as folls:
Cont until back meas 23.5(24.5,25.5,26.5) cm, ending with RS facing for next row.

Shape armholes
Keeping patt correct, cast off 4(5,6,6) sts at beg of next 2 rows. 107[119,129,141] sts.
Dec 1 st at each end of next 5(7,7,9) rows, then on foll 3(5,6,7) alt rows. 91[95,103,109] sts.
Cont straight until armhole meas 18(19.5,21,22.5) cm, ending with RS facing for next row.

Shape shoulders and back neck
Next row (RS): Cast off 5(5,5,6) sts, patt until there are 19(21,24,26) sts on right needle and turn, leaving rem sts on a holder.
Work each side of neck separately.
Dec 1 st at neck edge of 2nd and foll 4th row, **and at same time** cast off 5(5,5,6) sts at beg of 2nd row and 0(2,1,2) foll alt rows, then cast off 4(–, 6, –) sts on foll 2 (–, 1, –) alt row. 4[4,6,6] sts.
Work 1 row.
Cast off rem 4(4,6,6) sts.
With RS facing, slip centre 43(43,45,45) sts onto a holder, rejoin yarn to rem sts and patt to end.

Complete to match first side, reversing shapings.

FRONT

Work as given for back until 16(16,20,20) rows less have been worked than on back to beg of shoulder shaping, ending with RS facing for next row.

Shape front neck

Keeping patt correct work as folls:

Next row (RS): Patt 34(36,40,43) and turn, leaving rem sts on a holder.
Work each side of neck separately.
Cast off 3 sts at beg of next row, 2 sts at beg of foll 2 alt rows and 1 st at beg of 5(5,6,6) foll alt rows. 22[24,27,30] sts.
Work 0(0,2,2) rows straight.

Shape shoulder

Cast off 5(5,5,6) sts at beg of next and foll 1(3,2,3) foll alt rows, then 4(-, 6, -) sts at beg of foll 2 (-, 1, -) alt rows. 4[4,6,6] sts.
Work 1 row.
Cast off rem 4(4,6,6) sts.
With RS facing, slip centre 23 sts onto a holder, rejoin yarn to rem sts and cast off 3 sts, patt to end. 31[33,37,40] sts.
Complete to match first side, reversing shapings.

SLEEVES (make two the same)

Using 3.5mm (US 10/9) needles and yarn B cast on 43(45,47,47) sts.
Work 4cm, in rib as given for Back.
Break off yarn B, join in yarn A. Change to 4mm (US 6) needles.
Beg and ending rows as indicated, repeating the 16 st patt repeat twice across the row and repeating the 64 row patt repeat throughout (**please note:** sleeve incs are **NOT** shown on the chart), cont in patt as folls:
Inc 1 st at each end of 3rd and every foll 6th(6th,6th,4th) row to 55(65,77,53) sts, then on every foll 8th(8th,8th,6th) row until there are 75(79,85,89) sts, taking inc sts into patt.
Cont straight until sleeve meas 43(44,45,45) cm, ending with RS facing for next row.

Shape top

Keeping patt correct, cast off 4(5,6,6) sts at beg of next 2 rows. 67[69,73,77] sts.
Dec 1 st at each end of next 4(4,6,6) rows, then on 7(7,7,9) foll alt rows, then on 2 foll 4th rows. 41[43,43,43] sts.
Work 1 row, ending with RS facing for next row.
Dec 1 st at each end of next and 2(3,3,3) foll alt rows, then on foll 4 rows. 27 sts.
Work 1 row.
Cast off 3 sts at beg of next 2 rows, then 4

sts at beg of next 2 rows.
Cast off rem 13 sts.

MAKING UP

Press as described on the information page.
Join right shoulder seam using back stitch, or mattress stitch if preferred.

Neckband

With RS facing and using 3.5mm (US 10/9) needles and yarn B, pick up and knit 20(20,24,24) sts down left side of front neck, K across 23 sts on front holder, pick up and knit 20(20,24,24) sts up right side of front neck, 1 st down right side of back neck, K across 43(43,45,45) sts from back holder inc 1 st at centre and pick up and knit 1 st up left side of back neck. 109[109,119,119] sts.

Beg with row 2 of rib, work in rib as given for back for 2cm, with RS facing for next row. Cast off in rib.

Join left shoulder and neckband seams.
Set in sleeves.
Join side and sleeve seams.

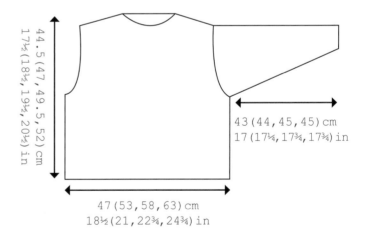

44.5(47,49.5,52) cm
17½(18½,19½,20½) in

43(44,45,45) cm
17(17¼,17¾,17¾) in

47(53,58,63) cm
18½(21,22¾,24¾) in

CHART

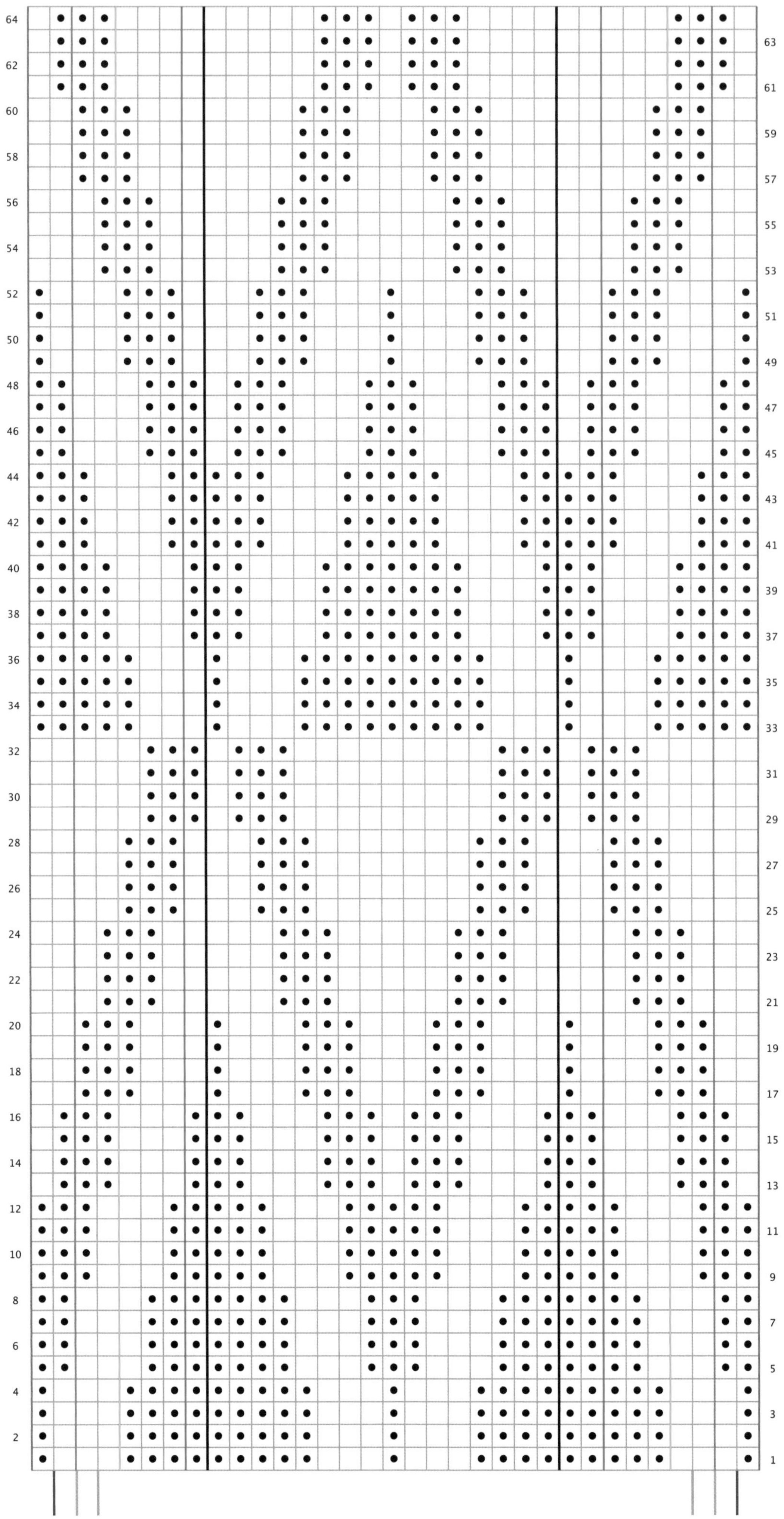

Key

	RS: knit WS: purl
●	RS: purl WS: knit
	16 st repeat
	S
	M
	L
	XL
	Sleeves S
	Sleeves M
	Sleeves L/XL

L/XL M S – Sleeves

Sleeves – S   M L/XL

CHEVRON
STATEMENT JUMPER

My Chevron jumper is a design I have been building in my head for quite a while now. The textured chevron pattern to the bottom half of the jumper perfectly echoes the deep v feature back neck. The unusual construction to the back is balanced with simple drop sleeves and neat side vents, creating the perfectly understated statement jumper.

SIZE

	S	M	L	XL	
To fit bust					
	81-86	91-97	102-107	112-117	cm
	32-34	36-38	40-42	44-46	in

Actual bust measurement of garment

104	116	124	133	cm
41	45¾	48¾	52½	in

YARN
Cocoon

8	9	9	10	x 100gm

(photographed in Dove 849)

NEEDLES
1 pair 6.5mm (no 3) (US 10) needles
6.5mm (no 3) (US 10) circular needle at least 100cm long.
1 pair 7mm (no 2) (US 10½) needles

EXTRAS
25-30cm of ribbon or trimming of your choice.
Stitch markers.
Stitch holders.

TENSION
14 sts and 16 rows to 10cm measured over st st, using 7mm (US 10½) needles.

RIGHT BACK
Using 6mm (US 10) needles cast on 34(38,40,44) sts.
Row 1 (RS): * K1, P1,rep from * to end.
Row 2: As row 1.

These 2 rows form rib.
Work in rib until right back meas 4 cm, inc — (-, 1, -) st in centre of last row and ending with RS facing for next row.
34[38,41,44] sts.
Change to 7mm (US 10½) needles.
Now work in patt as folls:
Row 1 (RS): K2, work next 32(36,39,42) sts from row 1 of chart.
Row 2: Work 32(36,39,42) sts from row 2 of chart, K2.
These 2 rows set the sts, chart sts with 2 g st sts at side edge.
Cont as set until chart row 40 has been worked, ending with RS facing for next row.
Place a coloured marker at side edge of last row (this is to denote the base of the side seam).
Beg with a K row, now work in st st until right back meas 50(52,53,55) cm, ending with RS facing for next row.

Shape back slope
Next row (RS): K to last 4 sts, K2tog, K2.
33[37, 40, 43] sts.
Work 1 row.
Working all back slope decreases as set by last row, cont
dec 1 st at slope edge of 3rd and foll 3(3,2,2) 4th rows, then on foll 7(7,9,9) alt rows. 22[26,28,31] sts.
Cont straight until left back meas 70(72,74,76)cm, ending with RS facing for next row.

Shape shoulder
Cast off 4(5,5,6) sts at beg of next and foll 2(3, 1, 3) alt rows, then 5(-, 6, -) sts at beg of foll 1 (-, 2, -) alt row.

Work 1 row.
Cast off rem 5(6,6,7) sts.

LEFT BACK
Using 6mm (US 10) needles cast on
34(38,40,44) sts.
Row 1 (RS): * P1, K1,rep from * to end.
Row 2: As row 1.
These 2 rows form rib.
Work in rib until left back meas 4 cm, inc —
(-, 1, -) st in centre of last row and ending
with RS facing for next row.
34[38,41,44] sts.
Change to 7mm (US 10½) needles.
Now work in patt as folls:
Row 1 (RS): Work 32(36,39,42) sts from row 1
of chart, K2.
Row 2: K2, work next 32(36,39,42) sts from
row 2 of chart.
These 2 rows set the sts, chart sts with
2 g st sts at side edge.
Cont as set until chart row 40 has been
worked, ending with RS facing for next row.
**Place a coloured marker at side edge of last
row (this is to denote base of the side seams)**
Beg with a K row, now work in st st until
left back meas 50(52,53,55) cm, ending with
RS facing for next row.

Shape back slope
Next row (RS): K2, Sl 1, K1, Psso, knit to
end. 33[37, 40, 43] sts.
Working all back slope decreases as set by
last row, complete to match right back,
reversing shapings.

FRONT
Using 6mm (US 10) needles cast on
75(83,89,95) sts.
Row 1 (RS): K1, *P1, K1, rep from * to end.
Row 2: *P1, K1, rep from * to last st, P1.
These 2 rows form rib.
Work in rib until front meas 4 cm, ending
with RS facing for next row.
Change to 7mm (US 10½) needles.
Now work in patt as folls:
Row 1 (RS): K2, work next 71(79,85,91) sts
from row 1 of chart, K2.
Row 2: K2, work next 71(79,85,91) sts from
row 2 of chart, K2.
These 2 rows set the sts, chart sts with 2 g
st sts at side edges.
Cont as set until chart row 40 has been
worked, ending with RS facing for next row.
**Place coloured markers at each end of last
row (this is to denote base of the side seams)**
Beg with a K row, now work in st st until
front is 4(4,6,6) rows less than right back
to shoulder shaping, ending with ending with
RS facing for next row.

Shape front neck
Next row (RS): K30(34,36,39) and turn,
leaving rem sts on a holder.
Work each side of neck separately.
Cast off 2 sts at neck edge of next and foll
alt row, then — (-, 1, 1) st at neck edge of
foll — (-, 1, 1) alt row. 26[30,31,34] sts.

Shape shoulder
Cast off 4(5,5,6) sts at beg of next and foll
2(3,1,3) alt rows, then 5(-, 6, -) sts at beg
of foll 1 (-, 2, -) alt rows, **and at same
time** cast off 2(2,1,1) sts at beg of 2nd row
and 1 st at beg of foll 2 alt rows.
Work 1 row.
Cast off rem 5(6,6,7) sts.
With RS facing, slip centre 15(15,17,17) sts
onto a holder, rejoin yarn to rem sts and
cast off 2 sts, K to end. 28[32,34,37] sts.
Complete to match first side,
reversing shapings.

SLEEVES (make two the same)
Using 6mm (US 10) needles cast on
33(35,37,37) sts.
Work in rib as given for back for 4cm, inc
1 st in centre of last row, ending with RS
facing for next row. 34[36,38,38] sts.
Change to 7mm (US 10½) needles.
Beg wih a K row, work in st st shaping sides
by inc 1 st at each end of next and every
foll 6th(6th,6th,4th) row to 54(54,54,48) sts,
then on every foll — (8th,8th,6th) row until
there are — (56,58,62) sts.
Cont straight until sleeve meas 43(44,45,45) cm,
ending with RS facing for next row.

Shape top
Cast off 5(5,5,6) sts at beg of next 4(2,2,6)
rows. 34[46,48,26] sts.
Cast off 6(6,6,7) sts at beg of next
4(6,6,2) rows.
Cast off rem 10(10,12,12) sts.

MAKING UP
Press as described on the information page.
Join both shoulder seams using back stitch or
mattress stitch if preferred.

Borders and neckband
With RS facing and using 6.5mm (US 10)
circular needle, beg and ending at cast-on
edges of backs, pick up 129(131,135,137) sts
up left back opening edge, 19(19,21,21) sts
down left front neck, knit 15(15,17,17) sts
from front neck holder, 19(19,21,21) sts up
right front neck and 129(131,135,137) sts
down right back opening edge.
311[315,327,331] sts.

Beg with row 2, work in rib as given for back for 4 rows, ending with **WS** facing for next row.

Now place right sides of band together, slide sts at both sides of hem to either end of the circular needle and work a three-needle cast off until beg of back V neck shaping, then separate the two sides of the band and continue casting off normally now and in rib, so you work up one side of back V-neck, across front neck and down the other side of back V-neck.

Place markers 20(21,22,23) cm below beginning of shoulder seam to denote armholes.

Sew in sleeves.
Join side seams from stitch markers.
Join sleeve seams.
Sew ribbon or trimming in place as shown in the photograph.

See information page for finishing instructions.

TIP: THREE NEEDLE CAST OFF
A three needle cast off is a way of joining two pieces of knitting that are still on the needles, that creates a seam whilst casting off.

With stitches arranged on your needles so that first stitches and last stitches of your rib are at each end of your circular needle respectively, place right sides of work together, wrong sides facing out, and needles held parallel together. Take a spare needle of the same size and insert it as if to knit, through the first stitch on both needles and knit them together at the same time. Do this again in the same way. Using one of your needles held parallel, pass the first stitch on your right hand needle over the second stitch and off the needle, just how you would when casting off. Continue in this way, as instructed, to join the live stitches together creating and seam and casting off at the same time.

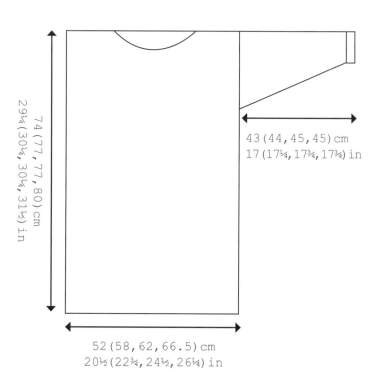

74(77,77,80)cm
29¼(30¼,30¼,31½)in

43(44,45,45)cm
17(17¼,17¾,17¾)in

52(58,62,66.5)cm
20½(22¾,24½,26¼)in

CHART

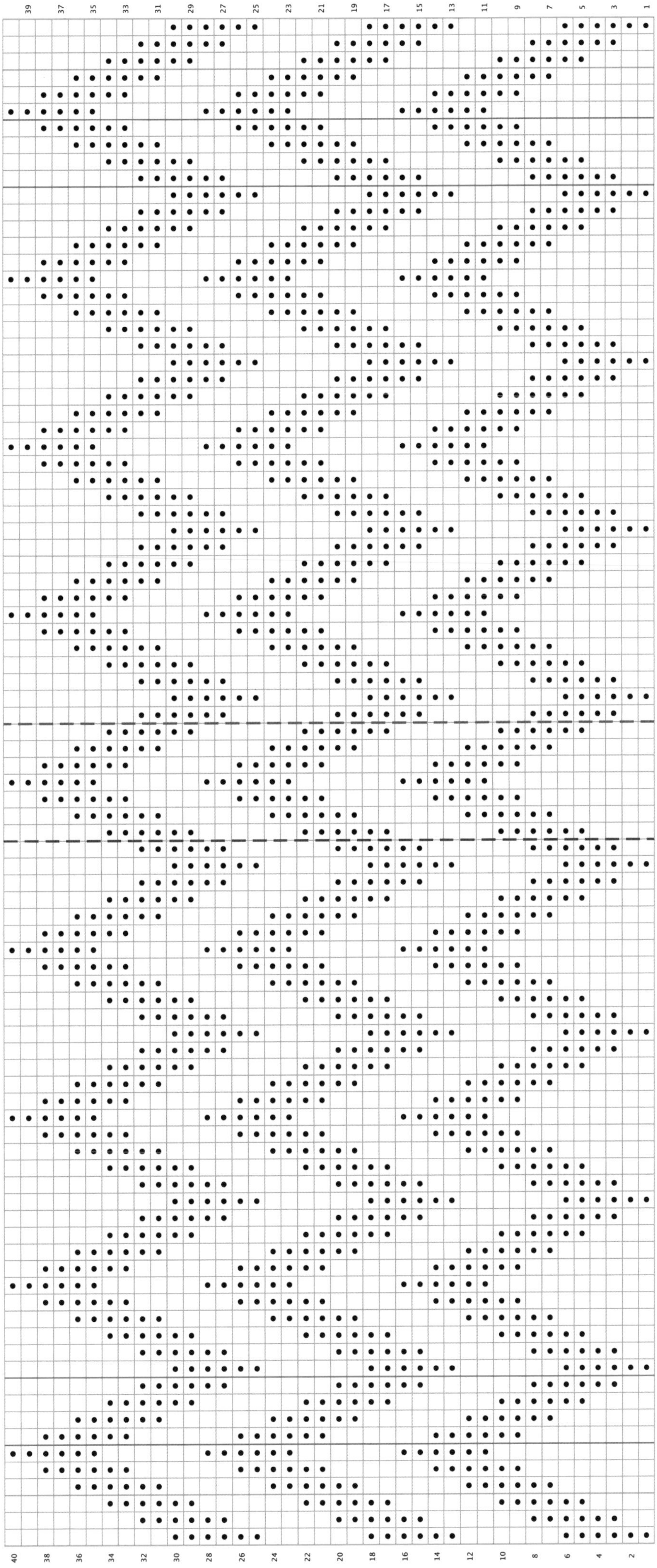

Key

	RS: knit WS: purl
•	RS: purl WS: knit
	S
	M
	L
	XL
	Left Centre Back
	Right Centre Back

HERON

PEPLUM JUMPER

Heron's textured body is inspired by a building I passed almost every day when I was studying, the Heron Tower in London, the peplum adds a fun twist to this boxy jumper.

SIZE

	S	M	L	XL	
To fit bust					
	81-86	91-97	102-107	112-117	cm
	32-34	36-38	40-42	44-46	in

Actual bust measurement of garment

108	115	122	130	cm
42½	45½	48	51	in

YARN
Kid Classic

9	10	11	12	x 50gm

(photographed in Drought 876)

NEEDLES
1 pair 6mm (no 4) (US 10) needles
1 pair 4.5mm (no 7) (US 7) needles
4.5mm (no 7) (US 7) circular needle,
40cm long
Cable needle

EXTRAS
Stitch markers.
Stitch holders.

TENSION
25 sts and 27 rows to 10cm measured over patt, 20 sts and 27 rows to 10cm measured over st st, both using 4.5mm (US 7) needles.

SPECIAL ABBREVIATIONS
T2F = slip next st onto cable needle and leave at front of work, P1, then K1 from cable needle; **Sl 1p wyif** = slip 1 stitch purlwise with yarn in front (**WS** of work).

BACK
Using 6mm (US 10) needles cast on 274(292,310,328) sts.
Beg with a K row, work 30 rows in st st.
Change to 4.5mm needles.
Next row: *K2tog, rep from * to end.
137[146,155,164] sts.
Next row: Purl.
Now work in patt as folls:
Row 1 (RS): P1, *P1, K8, rep from * to last st, K1.
Row 2: P1, *Sl 1p wyif, P6, Sl 1p wyif, K1, rep from * to last st, K1.
Row 3: P1, *P1, T2F, K6, rep from * to last st, K1.
Row 4: P1, *Sl 1p wyif, P5, Sl 1p wyif, K2, rep from * to last st, K1.
Row 5: P1, *P2, T2F, K5, rep from * to last st, K1.
Row 6: P1, *Sl 1p wyif, P4, Sl 1p wyif, K3, rep from * to last st, K1.
Row 7: P1, *P3, T2F, K4, rep from * to last st, K1.
Row 8: P1, *Sl 1p wyif, P3, Sl 1p wyif, K4, rep from * to last st, K1.
Row 9: P1, *P4, T2F, K3, rep from * to last st, K1.
Row 10: P1, *Sl 1p wyif, P2, Sl 1p wyif, K5, rep from * to last st, K1.
Row 11: P1, *P5, T2F, K2, rep from * to last st, K1.
Row 12: P1, *Sl 1p wyif, P1, Sl 1p wyif, K6, rep from * to last st, K1.
Row 13: P1, *P6, T2F, K1, rep from * to last st, K1.
Row 14: P1, *(Sl 1p wyif) twice, K7, rep from * to last st, K1.
Row 15: P1, *P7, T2F, rep from * to last st, K1.
Row 16: P1, *Sl 1p wyif, K8 rep from * to

last st, K1.
These 16 rows form patt.

Cont in patt until back meas 33(34,35,36) cm,
ending with RS facing for next row.

Shape for sleeve extensions
Cast on 1 st at beg of next 8 rows, 2 sts
on foll 4 rows, then 5(5,6,6) sts on foll 2
rows, and 12(12,13,13) sts on foll 2 rows.
187[196,209,218] sts.
Place markers at both ends of last row (to
denote base of sleeve openings).
Cont straight until sleeve meas
13.5(14.5,15.5,16.5) cm, ending with RS
facing for next row.

Shape shoulders
Cast off 7(7,8,8) sts at beg of next
10(4,10,2) rows, then — (8, -, 9) sts at beg of
foll — (6, -, 8) rows. 117[120,129,130] sts.

Shape back neck
Next row (RS): Cast off 7(8,9,9) sts, patt
until there are 26(26,29,29) sts on right
needle and turn, leaving rem sts on a holder.
Work each side of neck separately.
Dec 1 st at neck edge of next and foll alt
rows, **and at same time** cast off 8(8,9,9) sts
at beg of 2nd row and foll alt row.
Work 1 row.
Cast off rem 8(8,9,9) sts.
With RS facing, slip centre 51(52,53,54) sts
onto a holder, rejoin yarn and patt to end.
Complete to match first side,
reversing shapings.

FRONT
Work as given for back until beg of shoulder
shaping, ending with RS facing for next row.

Shape shoulders
Cast off 7(7, -, -) sts at beg of next
2(2, -, -) rows. 173[182,209,218] sts.

Shape front neck
Next row (RS): Cast off 7(7,8,8) sts, patt
until there are 65(69,82,86) sts on right
needle and turn, leaving rem sts on a holder.
Work each side of neck separately.
Cast off 4 sts at neck edge of next and 3 sts
at beg of foll 2 alt rows, then 2 sts at beg
of foll alt row, 1 st at beg of foll 1(1,2,2)
alt rows, **and at same time** cast off 7(8,8,9)
sts at beg of 2nd row and foll 3(5,3,6) alt
rows, then 8(-, 9, -) sts at beg foll
2 (-, 3, -) alt rows.
Work 1 row.
Cast off rem 8(8,9,9) sts.
With RS facing, slip centre 29(30,29,30) sts
onto a holder, rejoin yarn and patt to end.
Complete to match first side,
reversing shapings.

SLEEVES (make two the same)
Using 4.5mm (US 7) needles cast on
39(41,43,43) sts.
Cont in st st as folls:
Inc 1 st at each end of 5th and every foll
6th(6th,6th,4th) row to 51(55,63,57) sts, then
on every foll 8th(8th, -, 6th) row until there
are 55(59, -,67) sts.
Cont straight until sleeve meas
23.5(24.5,25.5,25.5) cm, ending with RS
facing for next row.

Shape top
Cast off 6(7,7,8) sts at beg of next 2(4,2,4)
rows. 43[31,49,35] sts.
Cast off 7(8,8,9) sts at beg of next
4(2,4,2) rows.
Cast off rem 15(15,17,17) sts.

MAKING UP
Press as described on the information page.
Block to finished measurements, taking care
not to block out the peplum but to pin
it down in folds and waves to maintain
its shape.
Join both shoulder seams using back stitch,
or mattress stitch if preferred.
Neckband
With RS facing and using 4.5mm (US
7) circular needle, pick up and knit
21(21,23,23) sts down left side of front
neck, K across 29(30,29,30) sts on front
holder, pick up and knit 21(21,23,23) sts up
right side of front neck, 5 sts down right
side of back neck, K across 51(52,53,54) sts
on back holder, pick up and knit 5 sts up
right side of back neck.
132[134,138,140] sts.

Place marker to mark beg of round.
Rounds 1 to 5: Knit.
Cast off.

Sew in sleeves.
Join side and sleeve seams, reversing sewing
for roll edge.

See information page for finishing
instructions.

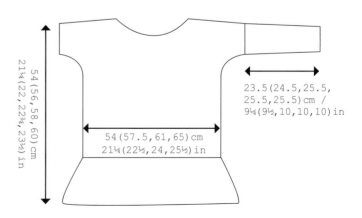

L.D.N.

CARDIGAN

Inspired by the rows and rows of windows that look out over London, that I gaze up at when I go walking looking for inspiration, my L.D.N. cardigan features a pattern of textured blocks and simple stripes to the bottom half before being divided into 3 sections and shaped out to create sleeves.

SIZE

	S	M	L	XL	
To fit bust					
	81–86	91–97	102–107	112–117	cm
	32–34	36–38	40–42	44–46	in

Actual bust measurement of garment

119	130	141	156	cm
47	51¼	55½	61	in

YARN
Cocoon
A Alpine 802

7	7	8	9	x 100gm

B Shale 804

1	1	1	1	x 100gm

C Petrol 846

1	1	1	1	x 100gm

NEEDLES
1 pair 7mm (no 2) (US 10½) needles
6mm (no 4) (US 10) circular needle at least 100cm long.

EXTRAS
Stitch holders.
Stitch markers.

TENSION
14 sts and 16 rows to 10cm measured over st st using 7mm (US 10) needles.

BODY (Worked in one piece until sleeve shaping)
Using 7mm (US 10½) needles and yarn A cast on 141(157,173,189) sts.
Work in g st for 8 rows. Beg with a K row, work 4 rows in st st.
Now work in patt as folls:
** Using yarn B, knit 2 rows.
Using yarn C, knit 2 rows.
Using yarn B, knit 2 rows.
Break off yarns B and C.
Using yarn A only and beg with a K row, work 4 rows in st st.
Row 11 (RS): Purl.
Row 12: Knit.
Row 13: P4, *K5, P3, rep from * to last st, P1.
Row 14: K1, *K3, P5, rep from * to last 4 sts, K4.
Rows 15 to 20: Rep rows 13 and 14, 3 times.
Row 21: Purl.
Row 22: Knit.
Beg with a K row, work 4 rows in st st. **
Rep from ** to ** once more.
Using yarn B, knit 2 rows.
Using yarn C, knit 2 rows.
Using yarn B, knit 2 rows.
Break off yarns B and C.
Using yarn A only work as folls:
Next row: K12(15,19,18), *M1, K13(14,15,17), rep from * to last 12(16,19,18) sts, M1, K12(16,19,18). 151[167,183,199] sts.
Beg with a P row, work in st st until work meas 35.5(36.5,37.5,38.5)cm, ending with RS facing for next row.
Working in st st throughout divide for back and fronts as folls:

RIGHT FRONT
Next row (RS): K34(38,42,45), and turn, leaving rem sts on a stitch holder.

Shape for Sleeve
Cast on 1 st at beg of next row, and at same edge on foll 3 alt rows, then 2 sts on foll 4 alt rows, 3 sts on foll alt row, then 5(5,6,6) sts on foll alt row, then 11(12,13,13) sts on foll alt row and 21(22,22,22) sts on foll alt row. 86[92,98,101] sts.
Place a coloured marker at side edge of last row (this is to denote the base of the side seam).
Cont straight until sleeve meas 11.5(12,12.5,13) cm, from marker, ending with **WS** facing for next row.

Shape shoulder
Cast off 7(8,8,8) sts at beg of next and foll 7(-,6,9) alt rows, then 6(7,7,7) sts at beg of foll 4(11,5,2) alt rows. 6[7,7,7] sts.
Cast off rem 6(7,7,7) sts.

BACK
With RS facing, rejoin to rem sts and work as folls for back:
Shape for Sleeves
Next row: Cast on 1 st, K83(91,99,109), turn leaving rem sts on stitch holder.
Next row: Cast on 1 st, P to end. 85[93,101,111] sts.
Cont to work on this set of sts only as folls:
Cast on 1 st at beg of foll 6 rows, then 2 sts at beg of foll 8 rows, 3 sts at beg of foll 2 rows, then 5(5,6,6) sts at beg of foll 2 rows, then 11(12,13,13) sts at beg of foll 2 rows and 21(22,22,22) sts at beg of foll 2 rows. 187[199,211,221] sts.
Mark each end of last row to denote base of sleeve openings.
Cont straight until sleeve meas 11.5(12,12.5,13) cm, from markers, ending with RS facing for next row.

Shape shoulders
Cast off 7(8,8,8) sts at beg of next 16(2,14,20) rows, then 6(7,7,-) sts at beg of foll 4(18,6,-) rows. 51[57,57,61] sts.
Shape back neck
Next row (RS): Cast off 6(7,7,7) sts, K until there are 14(16,16,16) sts on right needle and turn, leaving rem sts on a holder.
Work each side of neck separately.
Dec 1 st at neck edge of next 2 rows **at same time** cast off 6(7,7,7) sts at beg of 2nd row.
Work 1 row.
Cast off rem 6(7,7,7)sts.
With RS facing, slip centre 11(11,11,13) sts onto a holder, rejoin yarn and K to end.
Complete to match first side, reversing shapings.

LEFT FRONT
With RS facing, rejoin to rem sts and work as folls for left front:
Shape for Sleeve
Next row (RS): Cast on 1 st, K34(38,42,45). 35[39,43,46] sts.
Cast on 1 st at beg of 2nd row, and at same edge on foll 2 alt rows, then 2 sts on foll 4 alt rows, 3 sts on foll alt

row, then 5(5,6,6) sts on foll alt row, then 11(12,13,13) sts on foll alt row and 21(22,22,22) sts on foll alt row. 86[92,98,101] sts.
Mark end of last row to denote base of sleeve opening.
Cont straight until sleeve meas 11.5(12,12.5,13) cm, from marker, ending with **RS** facing for next row.

Shape shoulder
Cast off 7(8,8,8) sts at beg of next and foll 7(-,6,9) alt row, then 6(7,7,7) sts at beg of foll 4(11,5,2) alt row. 6[7,7,7] sts.
Cast off rem 6(7,7,7) sts.

MAKING UP
Press as described on the information page.
Join both shoulder seams using back stitch or mattress stitch if preferred.

BAND
With RS facing and using 6mm (US 10) circular needle and yarn B, beg and ending at cast-on edges, pick up 99(101,103,105) sts up right front opening edge, 5sts down right back neck, knit 11(11,11,13) sts from back neck holder, 5sts up left back neck and 99(101,103,105) sts down left front opening edge. 219[223,227,233] sts.
Working in g st work 3 rows in B, 2 rows in C, then 3 rows in B. Cast off knitwise (on a **WS** row).

SLEEVE EDGINGS (both alike)
With RS facing and using 6mm (US 10) needles and yarn C, pick up and knit 30(32,34,36) sts evenly along sleeve edge between markers.
Work 3 rows in g-st.
Join in yarn B, and work 2 rows more.
Break off yarn B. Using yarn C work 2 rows more.
Cast off knitwise (on a WS row)

Join underarm / side seams.

See information page for finishing instructions.

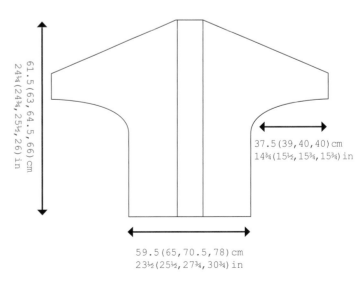

61.5(63, 64.5, 66) cm
24¾(24¾, 25¼, 26) in

37.5 (39,40,40) cm
14¾(15½, 15¾, 15¾) in

59.5(65, 70.5, 78) cm
23½(25½, 27¾, 30¾) in

STEEL STRUCTURES

LONGLINE CARDIGAN

The detail that runs around the bottom of this cardigan is actually inspired by a railway bridge that I spotted in East London one day when I was interning, the structural steel beams crossing and intersecting creating lines and shapes in the negative space really inspired me.

SIZE

	S	M	L	XL	
To fit bust					
	81-86	91-97	102-107	112-117	cm
	32-34	36-38	40-42	44-46	in

Actual bust measurement of garment

112	125	137	146	cm
44	49¼	54	57½	in

YARN

Brushed Fleece

9	10	11	12	x 50gm

(photographed in Hush 270)

NEEDLES

1 pair 6mm (no 4) (US 10) needles.
6mm (no 4) (US 10) circular needle at least 100cm long.
Cable needle.

EXTRAS

5 Buttons
Stitch holders
Stitch markers

TENSION

13 sts and 19 rows to 10cm measured over st st, 17 sts and 21 sts to 10cm measured over pattern, both using 6mm (US 10) needles.

SPECIAL ABBREVIATIONS

C4B = slip next 2 sts onto cable needle and leave at back of work, K2, then K2 from cable needle; **C3F** = slip next 2 sts onto cable needle and leave at front of work, K1, then K2 from cable needle; **C3B** = slip next st onto cable needle and leave at back of work, K2, then K1 from cable needle; **C3L** = slip next 2 sts onto cable needle and leave at front of work, P1, then K2 from cable needle; **C3R** = slip next st onto cable needle and leave at back of work, K2, then P1 from cable needle;

BODY (Worked in one piece to armholes)
Using 6mm (US 10) needles circular needle cast on 184(204,224,244) sts.
Work in patt as folls:
Row 1(RS): P1, (work 20 st repeat of chart) 9(10,11,12) times, P3.
Row 2: K1, (work 20 st repeat of chart) 9(10,11,12) times, K3.
These 2 rows set the sts — 9(10,11,12) cable panels with rev st st at sides.
Work a further 30 rows as set from Chart.
Next row (RS): K7(9,7,5), K2tog, (K2, K2tog) 42(46,52,58) times, K7(9,7,5).
141[157,171,185] sts.
Beg with a P row, work 15 rows in st st.

Pockets
Next row: K27 and turn.
Next row: P19 and turn.
Working on these 19 sts for first pocket work a further 50 rows in st st to form pocket lining.
Next row(RS): K19 sts of pocket lining, K106(122,136,150) sts across main piece and turn.
Next row: P19 and turn.
Working on these 19 sts for second pocket work a further 50 rows in st st to form pocket lining.

Next row: K across 19 sts of second pocket lining, K8.
Next row. Purl across all sts to end.
Working in st st throughout cont until work measures 47.5(48.5,49.5,50.5) cm, ending with RS facing for next row.

Shape front slope
Next row (RS): K2, Sl 1, K1, Psso, K to last 4 sts, K2tog, K2. 139[155,169,183] sts.
Working all front slope decreases as set by last row, dec 1 st at front slope edges of 4 (3, 4, -) foll 4th rows, then — (1,- ,3) foll 6th rows. 131[147,161,177] sts.
Work 3(1,1,1) rows straight.

Shape armholes and divide for back and fronts
Next row (RS): (K2, Sl 1, K1, Psso) —(-,1, -) times, K26(30,29,36), leave these sts on a holder, cast off 6(6,8,8) sts, knit until there are 67(75,81,89) sts on the right needle and slip these sts on to a holder, cast off 6(6,8,8) sts, K to last —(-,4, -) sts, (K2tog, K2) —(-,1, -) times. 26[30,33,36] sts.

LEFT FRONT
Next row (WS): Purl.
Dec 1 st at armhole edge on next 3(5,5,7) rows, then on foll 2(3,4,4) alt rows **and at same time** dec 1 st front slope edge of 1st(3rd,5th,3rd) and foll 1(1,1,2) 6th rows. 19[20,21,22] sts.
Dec 1 st at front slope edge **only** of 6th(4th,4th,6th) and foll 3(3,3,1) 6th rows, then foll -(-, -,1) 8th row. 15[16,17,19] sts.
Work 5[5,5,7] rows straight.

Shape shoulder
Cast off 4(5,6,6) sts at beg of next **and at same time** dec 1 st at front slope edge, then cast off 5(5,5,6) sts at beg of foll alt row.
Work 1 row.
Cast off rem 5(5,5,6) sts.

BACK
With **WS** facing, rejoin to rem 67(75,81,89) sts and work as folls for back:
Dec 1 st at each end of 2nd and 2(4,4,6) foll rows, then 2(3,4,4) foll alt rows. 57[59,63,67] sts.
Cont straight until back matches left front to beg of shoulder shaping, ending with RS facing for next row.
Shape shoulders and back neck
Next row (RS): Cast off 4[5,6,6] sts, K until there are 8(8,8,10) sts on right needle, K2tog, K2 and turn, leaving rem sts on a holder. 11[11,11,13] sts.
Work each side of neck separately.
Dec 1 st at neck edge **as before** of 2nd row **and at same time** cast off 5(5,5,6) sts at beg

of 2nd row. 5[5,5,6] sts
Work 1 row.
Cast off rem 5(5,5,6) sts.
With RS facing, slip centre 25(25,27,27) sts onto a holder, rejoin yarn and K2, Sl 1, K1, Psso, K to end. 15[16,17,19] sts.
Complete to match first side, reversing shapings.

RIGHT FRONT
With **WS** facing, rejoin to rem 26(30,32,36) sts and complete as given for left front, reversing shapings.

SLEEVES (make two the same)
Using 6mm (US 10) needles cast on 31(33,35,35) sts.
Cont in st st as folls:
Inc 1 st at each end of 7th(9th,7th,7th) and every foll 10th(10th,8th,8th) row to 47(49,43,51) sts, then on every foll - (-, 10th, 10th) row until there are -(-, 53, 55) sts.
Cont straight until sleeve meas 46(47,48,48) cm, ending with RS facing for next row.

Shape top
Cast off 3(3,4,4) sts at beg of next 2 rows. 41[43,45,47] sts.
Dec 1 st at each end of next 3 rows, then on 3(4,4,5) foll alt rows, then on 1(1,2,2) foll 4th rows. 27 sts.
Work 1 row, ending with RS facing for next row.
Dec 1 st at each end of next and foll 2 alt rows, then on foll 3 rows. 15 sts.
Cast off 4 sts at beg of next 2 rows. 7 sts.
Cast off rem 7 sts.

MAKING UP
Press as described on the information page.
Join both shoulder seams using back stitch or mattress stitch if preferred.

Front band
Using 6mm needles cast on 6 sts.
Row 1 (RS). (K1, P1) 3 times.
This row forms rib.
Cont in rib until front band, when slightly stretched fits up right front opening edge, from cast-on edge to beg of front slope shaping and sewing in place as you go along. Mark positions for 5 buttons on this section of band — first button to come 1.5cm up from cast-on edge, last button to come just below beg of front slope shaping, and rem 3 buttons evenly spaced between.

Cont in rib until band, when slightly

stretched, fits up right front slope, across
back neck, down left front slope, then left
front opening edge to cast-on edge, sewing in
place as you go along and with the addition
of 5 buttonholes in last section of band
worked to correspond with positions marked
for buttons as folls:
Buttonhole row (RS): K1, P1, Yrn, P2tog,
K1, P1.
When band is complete, ending with RS facing
for next row, cast off in rib.

Sew in sleeves.
Join sleeve seams.
Fold pocket linings in half and join
row-ends.
Sew on buttons.
See information page for finishing
instructions.

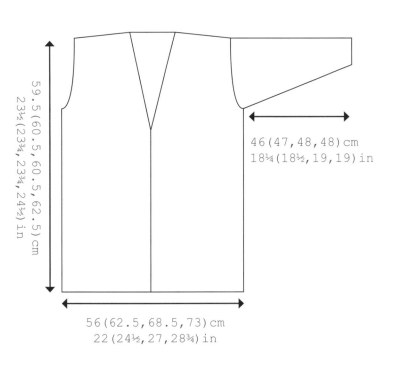

59.5(60.5,60.5,62.5)cm
23½(23¾,23¾,24½)in

46(47,48,48)cm
18¼(18½,19,19)in

56(62.5,68.5,73)cm
22(24½,27,28¾)in

CHART

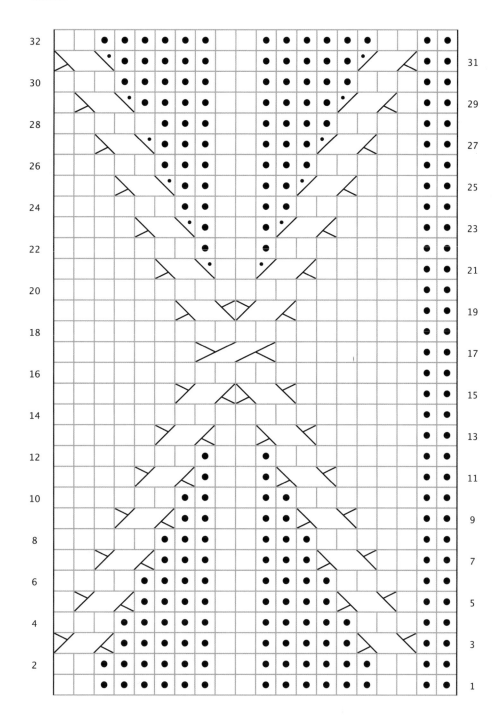

Key

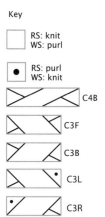

	RS: knit WS: purl
	RS: purl WS: knit
	C4B
	C3F
	C3B
	C3L
	C3R

T.O.

OVERSIZED JUMPER

T.O. is a perfectly oversized, chunky v-neck jumper with a textured pattern, inspired by the incredible, golden RBC towers I discovered whilst exploring Toronto.

SIZE

	S	M	L	XL	
To fit bust					
	81-86	91-97	102-107	112-117	cm
	32-34	36-38	40-42	44-46	in

Actual bust measurement of garment

112	124	131	143	cm
44	48¾	51½	56¼	in

YARN
Big Wool

9	10	11	12	x 100gm

(photographed in Pantomine 079)

NEEDLES
1 pair 9mm (no 00) (US 13) needles
1 pair 8mm (no 0) (US 11) needles

EXTRAS
Stitch markers

TENSION
10.5 sts and 18 rows to 10cm measured over patt, using 9mm (US 13) needles.

SPECIAL ABBREVIATIONS
Sl 1p wyif = slip 1 stitch purlwise with yarn in front (**WS** of work).

BACK
Using 8mm (US 11) needles cast on 61(67,71,77) sts.

Row 1 (RS): K1(1,0,0), *P2, K1, rep from * to last 0(0,2,2) sts, P0(0,2,2).
Row 2: K0(0,2,2), *P1, K2, rep from * to last 1(1,0,0) sts, P1(1,0,0).

These 2 rows form rib.
Work in rib for a further 4 rows, ending with RS facing for next row.
Change to 9mm (US 13) needles.
Beg and ending rows as indicated and repeating the 30 row patt rep throughout, now work in patt from Chart as folls:
Cont in patt until back meas 60.5(62.5,64.5,66.5)cm, ending with RS facing for next row.
Shape shoulder
Cast off 3(4,4,5) sts at beg of next and foll 5(7,5,7) rows, then 4(-,5, -) sts at beg of foll 2(-,2, -) rows. 35[35,37,37] sts.
Next row: Cast off 8 sts, patt until there are 19(19,21,21) sts on right hand needle, cast off rem 8 sts. (Neckband row-ends will be sewn to these 8 cast off sts later).
Leave 19(19,21,21) sts on a stitch holder.

FRONT
Work as given for back until 40(40,42,42) rows less have been worked than to beg of shoulder shaping, ending with RS facing for next row.
Divide for front neck
Next row (RS): Patt 28(31,33,36) sts, work 2tog and turn, leaving rem sts on a holder. 29[32,34,37] sts.
Work each side of neck separately.
Keeping patt correct, dec 1 st at neck edge on foll 6, 4th rows, then foll 7(7,8,8) alt rows. 16[19,20,23] sts.
Work 1 row.

Shape shoulder

Cast off 3(4,4,5) sts at beg of next and foll
2 alt rows, **at same time** dec 1 st at neck
edge of next and foll 2 alt rows.
Cast off rem 4(4,5,5) sts.
With RS facing, rejoin to rem sts, cast off
2 sts, patt end. 29[32,34,37] sts.
Complete to match first side, reversing
shapings.

SLEEVES

Using 8mm (US 11) needles cast on
27[27,29,29] sts.
Row 1 (RS): P1(1,2,2), K1, *P2, K1, rep from
* to last 1(1,2,2) sts, P1(1,2,2).
Row 2: K1(1,2,2), *P1, K2, rep from * to last
2(2,3,3) sts, P1, K1(1,2,2).
These 2 rows form rib.
Work in rib for a further 4 rows, ending with
RS facing for next row.
Change to 9mm (US 13) needles.
Beg and ending rows as indicated and
repeating the 30 row patt rep throughout, now
work in patt from Chart as folls:
Inc 1 st at each end of 3rd and every foll 4th
row to 31(35,35,41) sts, then on every foll
6th row until there are 51(53,55,57) sts,
taking inc sts into patt.
Cont straight until sleeve meas 44(45,46,46) cm,
ending with RS facing for next row.

Shape top

Cast off 5(5,6,6) sts at beg of next
2(2,8,8) rows. 41[43,7,9] sts.
Cast off 6(6, -, -) sts at beg of next
6(6, -, -) rows.
Cast off rem 5(7,7,9) sts.

MAKING UP

Press as described on the information page.
Join right shoulder seam using back stitch,
or mattress stitch if preferred.

Neckband

Using 8mm needles, pick up and knit
36(36,39,39) sts down left side of neck,
pick up 1 st at centre of V, pick up and
knit 36(36,39,39) sts up right side of neck.
73[73,79,79] sts.
Row 1 (WS): (P1, K2) 11(11,12,12) times,
P1, K2togtbl, P1, K2tog, P1, (K2, P1)
11(11,12,12) times. 71[71,77,77]sts.
Row 2: (K1, P2) 11(11,12,12) times, P2tog,
K1, P2togtbl, (P2, K1) 11(11,12,12) times.
69[69,75,75]sts.
Row 3: (P1, K2) 10(10,11,11) times, P1,
K1, K2togtbl, P1, K2tog, K1, P1, (K2, P1)
10(10,11,11) times. 67[67,73,73]sts.
Row 4: (K1, P2) 10(10,11,11) times,
K1, P2tog, K1, P2togtbl, K1, (P2, K1)
10(10,11,11) times. 65[65,71,71]sts.
Row 5: (P1, K2) 10(10,11,11) times,

P2togtbl, P1, P2tog, (K2, P1) 10(10,11,11)
times. 63[63,69,69] sts.
Cast off rem sts in patt, dec 1 st at either
side of V, then when you reach the end of the
neckband, continue casting off across sts left
on a stitch holder at centre back neck.

Join left shoulder seam. Sew row-ends of
neckband to 8 cast off sts at either side of
back neck. Place markers along side seam
edges 24(25,26,27) cm down from beg of
shoulder seams to denote armhole openings.

Sew in sleeves.
Join side and sleeve seams.
See information page for finishing instructions.

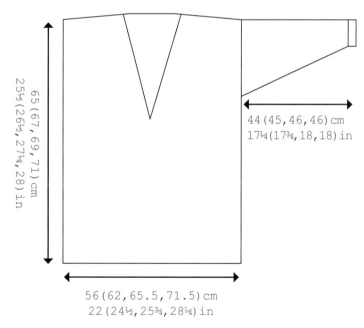

65 (67, 69, 71) cm
25½(26½, 27¼, 28) in

44 (45, 46, 46) cm
17¼(17¾, 18, 18) in

56 (62, 65.5, 71.5) cm
22 (24½, 25¾, 28¼) in

CHART

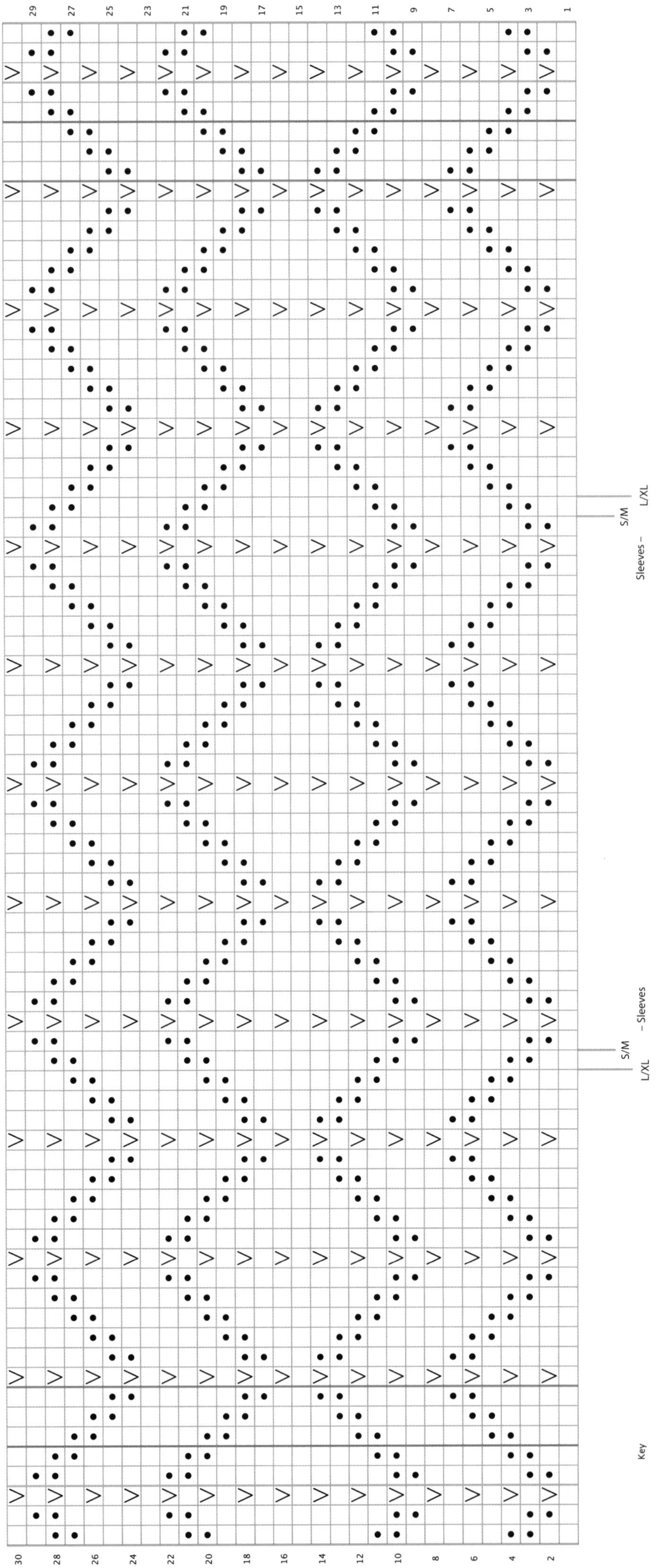

Key

	RS: knit WS: purl
•	RS: purl WS: knit
>	RS: slip WS: Sl 1p wyif
	S
	M
	L
	XL
	Sleeves S/M
	Sleeves L/XL

Sleeves – L/XL
S/M
Sleeves –

S/M – Sleeves
L/XL

ABBREVIATIONS

K — knit

P — purl

st(s) — stitch(es)

inc — increas(e)(ing)

dec — decreas(e)(ing)

st st — stocking stitch (1 row knit, 1 row purl)

g st — garter stitch (every row knit)

beg — begin(ning)

foll — following

rem — remain(ing)

alt — alternate

cont — continue

patt — pattern

tog — together

mm — millimetres

cm — centimetres

in — inch(es)

RS — right side

WS — wrong side

Sl 1 — slip one stitch

Sl 2tog — insert needle into next 2 sts as if to k2tog and slip the 2 sts from the left-hand needle to right-hand needle without working them.

Psso — pass slipped stitch over

P2sso — pass 2 slipped stitches over

M1 — make one stitch by picking up loop between last and next stitch and working into the back of this loop

Yrn — yarn round needle. Wrap yarn around the needle back to a purl position.

ROWAN STOCKISTS

AUSTRALIA: Australian Country Spinners, Pty Ltd, Level 7, 409 St. Kilda Road, Melbourne Vic 3004. Tel: 03 9380 3888 Fax: 03 9820 0989 Email: customerservice@auspinners.com.au

Morris and Sons 50 York Street, Sydney NSW 2000 Tel: 02 92998588

Morris and Sons Level 1, 234 Collins Street, Melbourne Vic 3000 Tel: 03 9654 0888

AUSTRIA: MEZ Harlander GmbH, Schulhof 6, 1. Stock, 1010 Wien, Austria Tel: + 00800 26 27 28 00 Fax: (00) 49 7644 802-133 Email: verkauf.harlander@mezcrafts.com

BELGIUM: MEZ crafts Belgium NV, c/o MEZ GmbH, Kaiserstr.1, 79341 Kenzingen Germany Tel: 0032 (0) 800 77 89 2 Fax: 00 49 7644 802 133 Email: sales.be-nl@mezcrafts.com

BULGARIA: MEZ Crafts Bulgaria EOOD, 7 Magnaurska Shkola Str., BG-1784 Sofia, Bulgaria Tel: (+359 2) 439 24 24 Fax: (+359 2) 976 77 20 Email: office.bg@mezcrafts.com

CANADA: Sirdar USA Inc. 406 20th Street SE, Hickory, North Carolina, USA 28602 Tel: 828 404 3705 Fax: 828 404 3707 Email: sirdarusa@sirdar.co.uk

CHINA: Commercial agent Mr Victor Li, c/o MEZ GmbH Germany, Kaiserstr. 1, 79341 Kenzingen / Germany Tel: (86- 21) 13816681825 Email: victor.li@mezcrafts.com

CHINA: Shanghai Yujun CO.LTD., Room 701 Wangjiao Plaza, No.175 Yan'an (E), 200002 Shanghai, China Tel: +86 2163739785 Email: jessechang@vip.163.com

CYPRUS: MEZ Crafts Bulgaria EOOD, 7 Magnaurska Shkola Str., BG-1784 Sofia, Bulgaria Tel: (+359 2) 439 34 24 Fax: (+359 2) 976 77 20 Email: marketing.cy@mezcrafts.com

CZECH REPUBLIC: Coats Czecho s.r.o.Staré Mesto 246 569 32 Tel: (420) 461616633 Email: galanterie@coats.com

DENMARK: Carl J. Permin A/S Egegaardsvej 28 DK-2610 Rødovre Tel: (45) 36 36 89 89 Email: permin@permin.dk

ESTONIA: MEZ Crafts Estonia OÜ, Ampri tee 9/4, 74001 Viimsi Harjumaa Tel: +372 630 6252 Email: info.ee@mezcrafts.com

FINLAND: Prym Consumer Finland Oy, Huhtimontie 6, 04200 KERAVA Tel: +358 9 274871

FRANCE: 3bcom, 35 avenue de Larrieu, 31094 Toulouse cedex 01, France Tel: 0033 (0) 562 202 096 Email: Commercial@3b-com.com

GERMANY: MEZ GmbH, Kaiserstr. 1, 79341 Kenzingen, Germany Tel: 0049 7644 802 222 Email: kenzingen.vertrieb@mezcrafts.com Fax: 0049 7644 802 300

GREECE: MEZ Crafts Bulgaria EOOD, 7 Magnaurska Shkola Str., BG-1784 Sofia, Bulgaria Tel: (+359 2) 439 24 24 Fax: (+359 2) 976 77 20 Email: office.bg@mezcrafts.com

HOLLAND: G. Brouwer & Zn B.V., Oudhuijzerweg 69, 3648 AB Wilnis Tel: 0031 (0) 297-281 557 Email: info@gbrouwer.nl

HONG KONG: East Unity Company Ltd, Unit B2, 7/F., Block B, Kailey Industrial Centre, 12 Fung Yip Street, Chai Wan Tel: (852)2869 7110 Email: eastunityco@yahoo.com.hk

ICELAND: Carl J. Permin A/S Egegaardsvej 28, DK-2610 Rødovre Tel: (45) 36 36 89 89 Email: permin@permin.dk

ITALY: Mez Cucirini Italy Srl, Viale Sarca, 223, 20126 MILANO Tel: 0039 0264109080 Email: servizio.clienti@mezcrafts.com Fax: 02 64109080

JAPAN: Hobbyra Hobbyre Corporation, 23-37, 5-Chome, Higashi-Ohi, Shinagawa-Ku, 1400011 Tokyo. Tel: +81334721104 Daidoh International, 3-8-11 Kudanminami Chiyodaku, Hiei Kudan Bldg 5F, 1018619 Tokyo. Tel +81-3-3222-7076, Fax +81-3-3222-7066

KOREA: My Knit Studio, 3F, 144 Gwanhun-Dong, 110-300 Jongno-Gu, Seoul Tel: 82-2-722-0006 Email: myknit@myknit.com

LATVIA: Latvian Crafts, 12-2, Jurģu street, LV-2011 Tel: +371 37 126326825   Email: vjelkins@latviancrafts.lv

LEBANON: y.knot, Saifi Village, Mkhalissiya Street 162, Beirut Tel: (961) 1 992211   Fax: (961) 1 315553   Email: y.knot@cyberia.net.lb

LITHUANIA: MEZ Crafts Lithuania UAB, A. Juozapaviciaus str. 6/2, LT-09310 Vilnius Tel: +370 527 30971   Fax: +370 527 2305 Email: info.lt@mezcrafts.com

LUXEMBOURG: MEZ GmbH, Kaiserstr.1, 79341 Kenzingen, Germany Tel: 00 49 7644 802 222 Email: kenzingen.vertrieb@mezcrafts.com

MEXICO: Estambres Crochet SA de CV, Aaron Saenz 1891-7Pte, 64650 MONTERREY TEL +52 (81) 8335-3870 Email: abremer@redmundial.com.mx

NEW ZEALAND: ACS New Zealand, P.O Box 76199, Northwood, Christchurch, New Zealand Tel: 64 3 323 6665 Fax: 64 3 323 6660 Email: lynn@impactmg.co.nz

NORWAY: Carl J. Permin A/S Egegaardsvej 28 DK-2610 Rødovre Tel: (45) 36 36 89 89 E-mail: permin@permin.dk

PORTUGAL: Mez Crafts Portugal, Lda – Av. Vasco da Gama, 774 - 4431-059 V.N, Gaia, Portugal Tel: 00 351 223 770700 Email: sales.iberia@mezcrafts.com

RUSSIA: Family Hobby, 124683, Moskau, Zelenograd, Haus 1505, Raum III Tel.: 007 (499) 270-32-47 Handtel. 007 916 213 74 04 Email: tv@fhobby.ruWeb: www.family-hobby.ru

SINGAPORE: Golden Dragon Store, 101 Upper Cross St. #02-51, People's Park Centre Tel: (65) 65358454 /65358234 Email: gdscraft@hotmail.com

SLOVAKIA: MEZ Crafts Slovakia, s.r.o. Seberíniho 1, 821 03 Bratislava, Slovakia Tel: +421 2 32 30 31 19 Email: galanteria@mezcrafts.com

SOUTH AFRICA: Arthur Bales LTD, 62 4th Avenue, Linden 2195 Tel: (27) 11 888 2401 Fax: (27) 11 782 6137 Email: arthurb@new.co.za

SPAIN: MEZ Fabra Spain S.A, Avda Meridiana 350, pta 13 D, 08027 Barcelona Tel: +34 932908400 Fax: +34 932908409 Email: atencion.clientes@mezcrafts.com

SWEDEN: Carl J. Permin A/S Egegaardsvej 28 DK-2610 Rødovre Tel: (45) 36 36 89 89 E-mail: permin@permin.dk

SWITZERLAND: MEZ Crafts Switzerland GmbH, c/o Puplicitas AG, Mürtenstrasse 39, 8048, Zürich Switzerland www.mezcrafts.com

TURKEY: MEZ Crafts Tekstil A.S, Kavacık Mahallesi, Ekinciler Cad. Necip Fazıl Sok. No.8 Kat: 5, 34810 Beykoz / Istanbul Tel: +90 216 425 88 10

TAIWAN: Cactus Quality Co Ltd, 7FL-2, No. 140, Sec.2 Roosevelt Rd, Taipei, 10084 Taiwan, R.O.C. Tel: 00886-2-23656527 Fax: 886-2-23656503 Email: cqcl@ms17.hinet.net

THAILAND: Global Wide Trading, 10 Lad Prao Soi 88, Bangkok 10310 Tel: 00 662 933 9019 Fax: 00 662 933 9110 Email: global.wide@yahoo.com

U.S.A.: Sirdar USA Inc. 406 20th Street SE, Hickory, North Carolina, USA 28602 Tel: 828 404 3705 Fax: 828 404 3707 Email: sirdarusa@sirdar.co.uk

U.K: Mez Crafts U.K, 17F Brooke's Mill, Armitage Bridge, Huddersfield, HD4 7NR Web: www.mezcrafts.com   Tel: 01484 950630

OTHER INFORMATION

TENSION

This is the size of your knitting. Most of the knitting patterns will have a tension quoted. This is how many stitches 10cm/4in in width and how many rows 10cm/4in in length to make a square. If your knitting doesn't match this then your finished garment will not measure the correct size. To obtain the correct measurements for your garment you must achieve the tension.

The tension quoted on a ball band is the manufacturer's average. For the manufacturer and designers to produce designs they have to use a tension for you to be able to obtain the measurements quoted. It's fine not to be the average, but you need to know if you meet the average or not. Then you can make the necessary adjustments to obtain the correct measurements.

YARN

Keep one ball band from each project so that you have a record of what you have used and most importantly how to care for your garment after it has been completed. Always remember to give the ball band with the garment if it is a gift.

The ball band normally provides you with the average tension and recommended needle sizes for the yarn, this may vary from what has been used in the pattern, always go with the pattern as the designer may change needles to obtain a certain look. The ball band also tells you the name of the yarn and what it is made of, the weight and approximate length of the ball of yarn along with the shade and dye lot numbers. This is important as dye lots can vary, you need to buy your yarn with matching dye lots.

PRESSING AND AFTERCARE

Having spent so long knitting your project it can be a great shame not to look after it properly. Some yarns are suitable for pressing once you have finished to improve the look of the fabric. To find out this information you will need to look on the yarn ball band, where there will be washing and care symbols.

Once you have checked to see if your yarn is suitable to be pressed and the knitting is a smooth texture (stocking stitch for example), pin out and place a damp cloth onto the knitted pieces. Hold the steam iron (at the correct temperature) approximately 10cm/4in away from the fabric and steam. Keep the knitted pieces pinned in place until cool. As a test it is a good idea to wash your tension square in the way you would expect to wash your garment.

THANK YOU'S

I would like to thank Rowan Yarns for their continued
support, the lovely team of knitters for their beautiful
workmanship, Jarek for his expert photography and Jill
for all her amazing technical hard work.

To the brilliant team at Quail, thank you for believing
in me and giving me the opportunity, freedom and support
to create my dream collection.

To all of my incredible friends, thank you for your
unending support. To Adam, thank you for making me laugh
when I was stressed, like only a brother can.

To my wonderful Nan,
thank you for teaching me
to knit and for putting
up with me when I dropped
all the stitches!

To my parents, thank you
for supporting me in
every single thing that
I do, you're simply
the best.

To Jordan, thank you for
always believing in me
and being there, for the
days spent walking around
London photographing
buildings with me and
for holding my yarn when
I'm knitting.